Love Beyond Death

Other Books by the Author

Voluptuously wrapped up in her death. Hans Makart, *The Death of Cleopatra*, 1874–75. (Staatliche und Städtische Kunstsammlungen Kassel, Neue Galerie.)

Love BEYOND Death

The Anatomy

of a Myth

in the Arts

Rudolph Binion

New York University Press
New York • London

NEW YORK UNIVERSITY PRESS
New York and London

Library of Congress Cataloging-in-Publication Data
Binion, Rudolph, 1927–
Love beyond death : the anatomy of a myth in the arts / Rudolph
Binion.
p.   cm.
Includes bibliographical references and index.
ISBN 0-8147-1189-8
1. Death in art.   2. Love in art.   3. Arts.   I. Title.
NX650.D4B55 1993   92-35152
700—dc20   CIP

New York University Press books are printed on acid-free paper,
and their binding materials are chosen for strength and durability.

Manufactured in the United States of America

c   10   9   8   7   6   5   4   3   2   1

Book design by Kathleen Szawiola

Dearest comrades, all is over and long gone.
But love is not over . . .
   —Walt Whitman, "Ashes of Soldiers"

Contents

Illustrations

Acknowledgments

*I*n preparing this book I incurred many debts. The late Roberta Recht shared in the research from start to near finish. I drew liberally on Joel Sheveloff's expertise in music and Alice Binion's in art. Marino Zorzi ran some rare books to ground for me. James Murphy located a lost painting for me. Robert Aldrich, Samuel Cohn, Jr., Bram Dijkstra, Stephen Kern, John Michael Montias, Robert Rosenblum, and Jack Spector gave the manuscript close critical readings at various stages. It also got a sound working over from Paul Elovitz's Psychohistory Forum. Most useful for my explorations of art were the Warburg Institute and the Witt Collection in London, the Bibliothèque Doucet and the documentation at the Louvre and the Musée d'Orsay in Paris, the Frick Library in New York, the Fogg Library at Harvard University, and the Biblioteca Germanica in Florence. Most useful all around were the British Library in London, the Bibliothèque Nationale in Paris, the Widener Library at Harvard University, the Österreichische Staatsbibliothek in Vienna, and the Marciana and the Querini-Stampaglia libraries in Venice. Brandeis University served my basic library needs and financed much of my travel. Finally, Raffael Scheck saw the book into print for me during my absence abroad, tying innumerable loose ends together in the process. Its merits are largely due to these several persons and institutions, but its faults are very much my own.

One

A Nineteenth-Century Phenomenon

*T*hroughout the nineteenth century plus a little before and after, high culture in the West was rife with visions of death as seductive and of sex and death intermixed. Here was no mere bumper crop of morbid fancies recurrent from time immemorial. Here was rather a whole new departure, which therefore calls for historical explaining.

Scholars have explored this new departure only in limited ways and without recognizing its newness. The closest approach to an overview of it for the whole period concerned is Mario Praz's stupendous, delectable, wrongheaded study of the taste for deathliness and evil in what he called romantic literature, primarily English, French, and Italian.[1] Praz saw this taste as a sickly literary fad with some weak precedents reaching back to the late Renaissance and with no historic significance outside of itself. He related its manifestations to algolagnia, or sadomasochism, in one author after another, though without ever generalizing the connection, let alone drawing on it to explain the phenomenon as a whole. Following Praz's lead, Philippe Ariès in his pioneering history of European attitudes toward death briefly argued an upsurge of violent and painful death in European art and letters since the late fifteenth century, with erotic underpinnings that gradually surfaced by about 1800.[2] And Michel Vovelle in turn in his massive, spotty history of death in the West barely alluded to a "link forged, or reinforced, between Eros and Thanatos" during the romantic period.[3] Other relevant monographs have been either far narrower in scope than Praz's or focused much farther afield from the love-death nexus.

Praz was wrong about algolagnia: death has been eroticized as often as not without a trace of cruelty. More importantly, although in the arts the conjunction of physical love with death was age-old, its sign switched in the late eighteenth century from negative to positive. That is, where traditionally in the arts death had been an ugly enemy of earthly, carnal love, now fleshliest love reconciled with death in all sorts of imaginary ways. This newfound partnership flourished in Western high culture until World War I, with a strong upsurge at the turn of the twentieth century. Then popular culture took it over, and its death component swelled gigantically. Such are the basic facts that comprise my subject.

The whys and wherefores of those facts will emerge piecemeal as I reconstruct them. To interpret in advance would carry no conviction. So I shall confine myself here to indicating that love beyond death, that fantasm fashioned by elites and then refashioned by mass culture, followed upon the collapse of implicit Christian faith by about 1800—of the simple assurance that our lives begin in sin and end in an eternal moment of truth. That simple faith collapsed even for professing Christians at the same time as Christian observances began falling off and Christian deconversions began multiplying. In the continuing aftermath of that huge collapse, post-Christian culture has picked up fragments of the old Christian creed in secular guises and disguises. One of those Christian fragments, spiritual love after death, reappeared in figurative art, creative literature, and music as the fleshly love-death mix.

Throughout my text as in my title I use the word "love" loosely to cover any erotic relationship, however impersonal. Erotism broke the death barrier in the arts beginning around 1775: for convenience I call whatever came before that break "premodern" and designate the whole time when this new development suffused culture from the top down, roughly 1775–1914, "the nineteenth century" for short. My subject being a single, huge point of contrast between premodern and modern culture as a whole, I intentionally ignore lesser chronological distinctions except for the 1914 divide. By the same token I also downplay secondary differentiating factors of culture such as nationality, religion, and schools of style. And I deliberately underinterpret the works I cite, being attentive to one thing alone: how they conjoined love and death.

One last, gigantic omission of no account: historic context. Nineteenth-century historiography developed the widespread, perhaps universal, notion that to explain any significant historic phenomenon or happening means to situate it with respect to a whole run of connected or connectible historic circumstances and to view it from a broad variety of interpretive angles. Accordingly, a mass Western fantasy shaping up towards 1800 and then building up until after 1900 would cry out for correlation with the concurrent growth of industry, cities, population, literacy, nationalism, the bourgeoisie, mass politics, mass consciousness, what have you. The going list of relevancies for that or any historic age keeps lengthening while the stress keeps shifting among them. A comprehensive approach is indeed imperative for the researcher intent on isolating specific causes in history. But then at the expository stage to bury such specific causality in all its attendant circumstances is self-defeating. In the present case the causality that I am advancing joins one mass fantasy, that of carnal love beyond death, to another that preceded it, that of spiritual love beyond death. And that causality alone is my subject.

My presentation has been dictated by my purpose. My purpose is, first, to establish the existence, and suggest the size and shape, of a nineteenth-century trend reconciling love with death that has hitherto been glimpsed only obliquely and inaccurately. To do this requires a generous sampling of the many and diverse linkages of love and death in the arts of the nineteenth century. My purpose is, further, to point up the discontinuity of that nineteenth-century trend with premodern associations of love and death in the arts, then to distinguish it qualitatively from its later, popular derivatives. That discontinuity can be shown more selectively than can the trend itself, and its later, popular derivatives will for their part be familiar enough to need little illustrating. The historic understanding of love beyond death implicit in all these demonstrations will be spelled out in conclusion. But first that fantasm must be set forth in its variety and its distinctiveness by turns, beginning with clustered specimens of the ways in which the prose and poetry, the painting, sculpture, and music of the nineteenth century coupled love and death.

From one such cluster to the next, that coupling in its matter-of-fact supernaturalism came slowly but surely to mimic a sacred myth.

Two

Its Variety

The nineteenth century was wont to join thoughts of love to thoughts of death. At the extreme, it might fuse the two outright into "loving death."[4] At lesser extremes it blended the two diversely. For Leopardi the prompt effect of love true and strong was "a desire to die."[5] The rhetoric of sex and death converged in Victorian novels[6] even as a veiled woman told a Victorian poet: "I and this Love are one—and I am Death!"[7] For Baudelaire, alcove and coffin were sisters in "frightful sweetness."[8] Flaubert tempted his Saint Anthony with Lust and Death speaking by turns and then singing a duet before finally fusing into a single figure.[9] The French fin de siècle did this duet to death—lovingly. "Love and death . . . the somber pit of the human soul," noted Émile Zola.[10] Female beauty made Albert Samain "dream of dying";[11] in Remy de Gourmont a lady told a new lover that her cloak would be "the survivor's shroud";[12] Jean Lorrain depicted Love and Death sowing and reaping hand in hand.[13] "Love and death are the same thing," declared an Octave Mirbeau heroine who purveyed both,[14] and Maurice Barrès noted: "Death and sensuality, pain and love, call each other up in our minds."[15] In the Germanies the relation was equally crisscross: love loomed deathly and death lovely for a young Hugo von Hofmannsthal or Thomas Mann.

Death for its own part, in and of itself, was alluring all century long. Novalis knew no joy to match "the enticements of death": its "rejuvenating gush" turned his blood to "balsam and ether."[16] Death obliged a youngster in Schubert with a cool, gentle caress.[17] Schubert's miller went "home" to "cool peace" in a whispering brook. And Schubert's winter wanderer heard a linden tree call him home from life, repeating: "Here you shall find your peace!"[18] Keats, oft "half in love with easeful death," yearned to "fade far away, dissolve," on hearing a nightingale sing.[19] Autumnal ripeness as Keats intoned it culminated in a swallows' requiem.[20] Heine, on hearing the nightingale's song, called death the cool night to the sultry day of life.[21] On Heine's rereckoning, "Life only warms / In death's cold arms."[22] Leopardi mused over "the kindness of dying."[23] For Lamartine's Raphaël, death resembled "a voluptuous absorption into the infinite."[24] Walt Whitman cherished "the low and delicious word death," which was "the word of the sweetest song."[25] The "strange need to feel dead" possessed a Jean Lahor drawn by the death deep in his mistress's eyes.[26] "The desire / To expire / Wells up in us like ecstasy," or again: "There are nights of mortal stress / When we dream of death to bless / Us with an infinite caress": thus Albert Samain craving "silence and oblivion in eternal rest."[27] Of the symbolists only Jules Bois ever repented a moment of being "drunk with dying."[28] Remy de Gourmont praised Pierre Louÿs's *Aphrodite* for ending like Chateaubriand's *Atala* with interlocked images of beauty and death slowly fading.[29] "Death is the highest expression of my sensuality," declared a Rachilde hero.[30] For Rilke, "The great death each of us bears deep within: / That is the fruit around which all things turn."[31] Renée Vivien, less inward, proclaimed: "I relish the violent taste of death."[32] Death sounded through the finale of Mahler's Ninth Symphony, and again the adagio of his unfinished Tenth, as a rapturous stillness.[33] Georg Heym thought it sweet to dream "of dissolving into light and earth, / Of being nothing more," for "Death is gentle. And gives us the home / That no one gave."[34] The end of this grave line was Wallace Stevens's "Death is the mother of beauty; hence from her / Alone shall come fulfillment to our dreams / And our desires."[35] "I would like to die, to be dead," began Giovanni Pascoli's elegies that ended with images of white-clad maidens dancing: "They speak and sing of love."[36] If this soft note of love enhanced the appeal of death for a Pascoli, how much headier was a Baudelaire's, a Swinburne's, a D'Annunzio's massive sexualization of that fatal lure.

That lure inhered in death of all descriptions, even hideous or merely prosaic. The popular Gothic novel heaped up corpses. The casual ghastly touch was modishly romantic, as when a rain cloud "spread its shroud over the whole sky."[37] Mary Shelley's Frankenstein fashioned his famed murderous monster out of human carrion.[38] Poe fashioned the murder mystery, thenceforth irresistible, out of a savaged corpse on the Rue Morgue.[39] Browning's masterpiece, *The Ring and the Book*, rhymed a dozen versions of a gruesome murder.[40] Goya and Géricault, followed by scores of imitators, depicted executions, dismemberments, severed heads and limbs galore.[41] Antoine Wiertz painted a live burial.[42] Paul Busson recounted how such a burial felt.[43] Pétrus Borel described a dead heroine decomposing.[44] A favorite early salon photograph was of a woman expiring.[45] Artists Maximilian Lenz, Albert von Keller, and Paul Albert Besnard documented women upon women agonizing or agonized.[46] James Ensor and Max Klinger imaged the macabre surreally. Edvard Munch pictured the living as spectral.[47] So did Jakob von Hoddis in apocalyptic verse.[48] Deathly women peopled Maximilián Pirner's canvases in fin-de-siècle Prague. Hugo Wolf composed a song for a dead man's voice.[49] Gottfried Benn cut his poetic eyeteeth on the charnel house.[50] And Georg Heym rhymed his placid way through corpse-filled rivers and ditches, fields and forests, cemeteries and hospitals and cities[51]—pending the great bloodbath of 1914–18.

Fascinating against all odds, death conferred so fetching a glamour throughout that same long century that any fair sampling under this rubric must run on and on. Very dead, yet only the more winsome, was limp Cordelia bemoaned by King Lear in James Barry's painting of 1786–88. Eerily enticing was Chateaubriand's amorous suicide Atala in Girodet's 1808 painting of her moonlit burial. Drowned Ophelia, already celebrated in pseudonymous Bonaventura's *Night Watches* of 1804, cast over the new century what Chateaubriand called "the spell of an enchantment."[52] She was to drift through Rimbaud's verse "on the calm black wave where the stars sleep,"[53] through Jean Lorrain's "beneath the sea-green water's tepid swirl,"[54] through Georges Rodenbach's enmeshed in a green flaxen tangle,[55] through Georg Heym's nibbled by muskrats while heading seawards to eternity.[56] Repeatedly Delacroix left off goring female flesh in effigy to draw, paint, or engrave Ophelia instead.[57] John Everett Millais showed her floating and chanting in ethereal rapture amidst her fantastic garlands in a weeping brook.[58] Albert Ciamberlani made her a gorgeous redhead,[59] Odilon Redon a wan shadow of her flowers.[60] Auguste Préault did a relief of her in an ecstasy of death,[61] and Sarah Bernhardt did one in her own spectral likeness.[62] Akin to Ophelia was a maiden of old Taranto drowned while sailing to join her fiancé: from a dirge by André Chénier[63] she went, delectably supine, into a statue by Pierre Alexandre Schoenewerk[64] (modeled on Auguste Clésinger's sexily gyrate *Woman Bitten by a Snake*).[65] *Found Drowned* by George Frederick Watts was perforce a comely female.[66] A death mask of a gorgeous drowned woman with eyes closed, smiling "as if she knew,"[67] sold along the Paris quais in the early 1900s. A painters' favorite after midcentury was spurned Elaine on her watery bier from Tennyson's *Idylls of the King*.[68] Another such around 1900, waterless now, was Albine on a bed of flowers, dead in ecstasy from their thick scent, out of Zola's *The Sin of Father Mouret*[69]— and dead Albine threw back to Gautier's wicked Clarimonde, who from beneath her white burial shroud aroused a priest's lust with her look of a spotless snowmaiden slumbering.[70] At the century's end a Barrès narrator saw in an Oriental courtesan mauled to death the epitome of the voluptuous—"eternal Helen."[71] An Occidental courtesan dead on the job highlighted the Salon of 1901 in Paris.[72] More soulfully Pierre Louÿs told of the nymph Byblis beautified forever by her death from amorous grief.[73] A 1900-ish "cult of the woman as corpse"[74] peaked pictorially in Romaine Brooks's chalky, skinny dead Venus stretched out in the middle of nowhere.[75] But the locus classicus for woman graced by death was Rossetti's lost love glowing trancelike out of his *Beata Beatrix*.[76] Death-graced males were in shorter supply. Walt Whitman mourned battlefield casualties: "sweet, ah sweet, are the dead with their silent eyes."[77] Henry Wallis painted a dead Chatterton girlishly pretty,[78] and Edward Onslow Ford sculpted a dead Shelley all in effeminate softness.[79] Only Rilke caressed the dead sexlessly through tender verses: "Their eyes have doubled back behind their lids / And now look inward."[80]

Dying could confer just as much fetching glamour as did death. In a Barbey d'Aurevilly of the 1830s the mere touch of a moribund heroine's feeble, feverish hand set a hero's bone marrow tingling.[81] In a little tragedy by Pushkin a crazed reveler sang a toast to a raging plague: "The baneful breath / Of dying beauty's our delight."[82] Poe took up the refrain: "I could not love except where Death / Was mingling his with Beauty's breath."[83] Calling the death of a beautiful woman the most poetic of subjects,[84] Poe depicted it ever more insistently from "Ligeia" through "For Annie" to his tombic love that was more than love in "Annabel Lee."[85] America's maudlin sweethearts at midcentury were dying Little Nell in *The Old Curiosity Shop* by Dickens, then dying Little Eva of *Uncle Tom's Cabin*;[86] a generation later both had yielded to untouchable pale lovelies expiring, as in Henry James from *Daisy Miller* to *The Wings of the Dove*.[87] Meanwhile, in Europe at midcentury a young poet struck a resounding note: "I love her for her funerary grace"[88]—and a generation later Maurice Rollinat tenderly sang of a "macabre mistress" bidding her lovers adieu and a "skeletal miss" who hanged herself.[89] Agonizing beauty came in bulk on canvas in Rollinat's day: witness Tony Robert-Fleury's *The Last Days of Corinth*, Georges Rochegrosse's *The Last Days of Babylon*, Aristide Sartorio's *Diana of Ephesus and the Slaves*.[90] Toward the century's end a Barrès hero told his fading beloved: "how I desire you beneath this pallor and redness of death!"[91] And Renée Vivien doted in verse on women in extremis exuding "agony and love."[92]

Deathlikeness competed for sex appeal with death and dying. Romantic night watchman Bonaventura swooned when he espied a "pale face . . . at once deathlike and loving" on one of his rounds.[93] Balzac's Raphaël relished the lifeless look of his mistress asleep.[94] As good as dead on canvas, or even better, were Girodet's dreamy Endymion,[95] Guérin's sleeping Cephalus,[96] Picot's somnolent Psyche,[97] or Delacroix's languid Odalisque, her thighs pruriently parted.[98] Life hung by a thread in Lord Leighton's torpid Ariadne.[99] The English excelled indeed at titillating torpidity: thus Leighton from *Ariadne* through *Summer Moon* and *Summer Slumber* to *Flaming June*,[100] John Frederick Lewis in *The Siesta*,[101] Albert Moore in *Beads, Apples, Dreamers*, or *Midsummer*,[102] Alfred Gilbert in *The Enchanted Chair*,[103] Edward Burne-Jones with his sleeping beauties, culminating in *The Sleeping Princess* stretched out as if in state.[104] Back on the continent, Alphonse Mucha posed his lush *Lying Model* face down to look like a dying model.[105]

With such inherent sexiness, death was a piquant aphrodisiac. Monk Lewis's wicked Ambrosio set the style by raping his kid sister in a crypt amidst rotting corpses.[106] Chateaubriand broke new mortuary ground with his Amélie declaring her passion for her brother in a Carmelite coffin on taking nun's vows; her brother clasped her to his bosom, winding sheet and all, crying: "Chaste bride of Jesus, receive my last embrace through the chill of death."[107] Delacroix blazed further carnal-charnel trails with lordly Sardanapalus watching the slaughter of his women (and horses) before his funeral pyre.[108] Poe could create erotic tension out of sheer deathliness, as with cadaverous Madeline Usher.[109] Baudelaire, who got erotic mileage out of a rotting carcass,[110] projected a poem to be titled "The Seductive Undertaker."[111] Swinburne reveled in a dead leper: "Love bites and stings me through to see / Her keen face made of sunken bones."[112] An impending ritual murder touched off "an orgy of prostitution" in Flaubert's *Salambô*.[113] Barrès saluted in budding Rachilde, darling of the decadents, her affinity for "those forms of love that smell of death."[114] Maupassant told of graveside prostitution in Paris;[115] Marcel Schwob, in old France;[116] Barrès, in Italy.[117] Schwob mated an executioner's daughter with a murderer in the storage room for the guillotine.[118] Iwan Gilkin paid poetic tribute to a virginal nurse turned on by deep surgery and death spasms.[119] An Octave Mirbeau heroine who got her thrills from painful executions recited to a gangrenous prisoner his own love poem "hymning the morbid beauty of decay."[120] And in Jean Lorrain it took a woman smelling of putrescence to arouse a "lover of death" whose icon was an Astarte with a death's head atop oversized genitals.[121]

Especially titillating was any and all imaginary erotic traffic between the living and the dead. In Sade's *Juliette* a father raped his disinterred daughter, decapitating her as he climaxed, and for the finale the heroine incited four rascals to sodomize her prissy sister's corpse.[122] Sade was with the century ahead. In a romantic ballad a knight violated a dead maiden, then thrice three moons later found a newborn babe at her rotted breast: "For love is to strength everlasting a friend / That gayly and swiftly draws life to its end / In the grave."[123] (A decadent was to top this with a girl who, pregnant by her brother, parturated after burying herself alive with him.)[124] In one of his loveliest lyrics Heine forwent all the world's joys to caress a corpse; in another he told his love he would nestle up to her dead body; in a third a dead youth took a sweetheart into his grave.[125] A girl received her dead beau nightly in Mickiewicz and again in Justinus Kerner.[126] Wicked dead nuns ensnared the hero of Meyerbeer's opera *Robert le diable*.[127] A legend of dead fiancées beside their graves waylaying men at night found its way through Hugo and Gautier into Adolphe Adam's ballet *Giselle*.[128] "Where are our loving ladies?" asked Gérard de

Nerval and answered: "In the tomb."[129] A voice reminded Flaubert's Saint Anthony how, on his deathwatch over the daughter of Martiallus, "desire shot through your veins like lightning."[130] Lust in person later told Anthony about an Egyptian embalmer jumping comely she-corpses "like a tiger."[131] Gautier fabled an Egyptologist in love with a maiden mummy[132]—and Hanns Heinz Ewers later made it a prehistoric Siberian princess preserved long ages in ice only to melt in a posthumous admirer's arms.[133] In a midcentury German classic a Roman legionnaire dug in with a fair corpse washed up by the Rhine.[134] Rossetti's dead love's lips "bubbled with brimming kisses at my mouth" in a woodside spring.[135] A French rhymer celebrated the nocturnal exploits of a dead-ladies' man.[136] Worth a thousand words and more was Gabriel von Max's painting of a professorial anatomist ever-so-properly unsheathing and ogling a luminous female cadaver stretched out on his dissecting table.[137] Rachilde's first heroine worked over her dead lover with gilt pincers, velvet-bedecked hammer, and silver scissors:[138] coitus with corpses wasn't for women. And when a modern-day Ishtar died of venereal deprivation in a novel of the same decadent decade, her husband, in hopes of reviving her, let her lover take her at last.[139]

Less patent dealings by the living with the dead could be all the more suggestive, as in Poe—loving a late spouse through her posthumous daughter while her tomb stands empty,[140] or gravitating to her sepulcher unmindful of her death.[141] In Poe again, a hated second wife, in dying, turned into her late lamented predecessor overnight,[142] and a husband drew his wife's teeth in a daze hard upon her premature burial.[143] An epigone of Poe's haunted heroes was Maupassant's madman in love with an antique lock of lady's hair because it at least was proof against decomposition.[144] A necrophiliac staple was the maiden impregnated while mistaken for dead, as in Otto Ludwig's *Maria*.[145] Equivalents were many: a woman raped in a dead faint in a novella by Kleist,[146] a robot girl wooed and wed in a tale by Hoffmann,[147] a sleepwalker violated in a Barbey d'Aurevilly.[148] Or a ravished statue: a Heine hero was stuck on a marble goddess he had kissed as a child,[149] a bridegroom in Mérimée perished upon spending his wedding night with a statue of Venus,[150] Sacher-Masoch's original masochist too made love to a marble Venus,[151] a sculptor in Zola hugged the head off his statue of a bathing beauty,[152] Oscar Wilde's swallow died kissing a prince's statue,[153] and in Henri de Régnier a sculpted narcissistic beauty drove men to their death until the sculptor hacked it to bits, kissing it on the lips for good measure.[154] An early poem by Oscar Wilde in this series was a double header: Athena drowned a youth for making love to her statue, whereupon a nymph died of passion for his corpse washed ashore.[155] On another necrophiliac tack, a uxorious widowed count in Villiers de l'Isle-Adam locked himself in with the memory of his wife until one night she revisited him in the flesh, leaving the keys to her crypt behind.[156] Equally spooky were Dr. Frankenstein's dream that in embracing his fiancée "I held the corpse of my dead mother in my arms"[157] and Heine's dream that a king's child he courted turned out to be dead.[158] So were a satanic seductress's claim in Huysmans to sleep with dead Byron, Baudelaire, or Nerval at will[159] and a Rachilde hero's thrill on entering his dying mistress's mother's tomb.[160] Fuseli depicted a wife locked up by her husband with her lover's skeleton;[161] fin-de-siècle Jean Lorrain upped it to three lovers' heads, their lips poisoned.[162] Young Flaubert likened a seasoned whore in action to "a dead woman awaking in love."[163] Baudelaire apostrophized another such whore: "Your carcass has its delights!"[164] Whitman eulogized a whore in the morgue: "Dead house of love . . ."[165] The living might caress the dead unintentionally: night watchman Bonaventura relished the sight of a man dead in his sleeping wife's arms.[166] Was Dickens spoofing this whole line of goods in naming an "articulator of human bones" Mr. Venus?[167]

What about sex among the dead? That perspective opened up with Gottfried Bürger's *Lenore* of 1773, a ballad of a soldier who returns from the wars to carry off his bride to their wedding: on arrival he turns into a skeleton as the earth swallows them up. Bürger's ballad enchanted Madame de Staël, Shelley, and Stendhal; Scott, Mickiewicz, and Nerval translated it; Hugo rewrote it; Ary Scheffer, Horace Vernet, and Jan Toorop illustrated it.[168] French pornography fed the same fancy less scarily: a specimen of 1793 featured a whole brothel enacting Elysian sexual antics around a client tricked into thinking himself dead.[169] After 1800 that game was played for real, and incessantly. Dead lovers haunted a night watch of Bonaventura, one of them affirming: "Only she who lives dies; she who is dead stays with me, and eternal is our love and our embrace."[170] A knowing ghost in Zacharias Werner had it that "Life is for love just a game; / Death is the way to love's aim."[171] Justinus Kerner versified a midnight tryst between two skeletons who declared: "To life we now attain at last in death!"[172] Clemens Brentano rhymed a devil investing a newly deceased virgin.[173] In death-ridden Thomas Lovell Beddoes, "they who pass, / In summer evenings, hear unearthly sighs" from a couple buried together.[174] The dead sang of passersby in Beddoes: "They would envy our delight, / In our graves by glow-worm night."[175] A ghost in Beddoes wooed a lady fair at her pillow: "Young soul, put off your flesh and come / With me into the quiet tomb, / Our bed is lovely, dark, and sweet."[176] And a dead lover in Beddoes, hinting of things to come, sent his live love a kiss through another's lips "For thee to taste and then to die."[177] Musset had a woman implore death to let her hold her lover's hand in the grave.[178] Élisa Mercoeur welcomed death for reuniting her with her lover.[179] Heine looked forward to lying buried in his love's arms while other corpses would dance at midnight.[180] A composer's dead love leading a frenetic rondo around his grave was the stuff of a Berlioz symphony.[181] Corpses mated by moonlight in the verses of imaginary romantic Élie Mariaker.[182] Büchner's Danton apostrophized his Julie: "You sweet grave, your lips are funeral bells, your voice my death knell, your breast my burial mound, and your heart my coffin."[183] Büchner's more jovial Leonce, asked by his betrothed if he would love her forever, replied obligingly: "I shall love your corpse."[184] Flaubert in his boyhood enjoined the dead with bitter rapture: "Kiss! Your mouths no longer bite . . . kiss while thinking of the lost joys of the earth."[185] Emily Brontë's Heathcliff, haunted by his Cathy's ghost, bribed a sexton to remove a panel of her coffin so that he could bury himself against her.[186] Elizabeth Barrett Browning, having counted the ways she loved thee alive, added: "If God choose / I shall but love thee better after death."[187] Hugo dreamed of eternal death with a sweetheart.[188] Baudelaire yearned to kiss his demoness all over in a sleep of death.[189] Baudelaire's dying lovers looked forward to "couches deep as tombs,"[190] while to Georg Heym's the sea itself sang: "We shall remain beside each other always."[191] In Marcel Schwob a dead girl of old Egypt schemed to get her sister's beloved buried beside herself.[192] An adulteress in Remy de Gourmont dreamed of an eternity of caresses by "perverse angels."[193] Black magician Aleister Crowley prayed: "Now let me die, to mate in hell / With thee, o harlot Jezebel."[194] In art meanwhile Émile Hébert sculpted a male cadaver risen from the grave to clutch a freshly fading female.[195] George

Frederick Watts imaged one nude couple at Mammon's feet and another at a rejoicing angel's.[196] Georges Lacombe carved a pair of lovers into a wooden coffin-bed.[197] And red hot was the molten landscape in Jean Delville's *Satan's Treasures*, with its interlaced corpses streaming under the fallen angel's fiery limbs.[198]

Extremes of mourning blended into the carnal-charnel composite. Wanting a dead love back or, better, wanting to follow one into death went on lavish literary display, with a premium on wallowing in grief. A consecrated romantic image was dying, like Hugo's Quasimodo, on a beloved's grave.[199] Many a tale already cited, such as Poe's "Ligeia" or Villiers de l'Isle-Adam's "Véra," was a showcase of fixation on a dead wife. French pornography paid this motif comic homage under the Terror with a bereft lover doing his brothel business beside his mistress's mummy.[200] By contrast, Novalis religified his craving to join his dead love after having sighted her through the tomb by night, transfigured.[201] Pathetically, a graveside lover in Bonaventura embraced his beloved's evanescent ghost.[202] Hebel told of a coal miner's carbolic-acid-drenched corpse turned up intact at the end of his fiancée's lifetime of mourning: she celebrated his funeral as a wedding.[203] Byron's Giaour begged an apparition of his murdered Leïla to contrive their speedy reunion.[204] Heine in his verses dreamed again and again of a dead love returning, or of his kissing her, or of her watching him, and he caressed her in her tomb till he became a corpse beside her.[205] In Poe a ship's passenger escorting his wife's coffin drowned himself with it in his insuperable sorrow.[206] Exhuming a beloved's corpse in a paroxysm of grief was common practice pictorially and especially literarily, as in *Camille* by Dumas fils[207] or "The Tomb" by Maupassant.[208] Melville's Taji pursued his lost Yillah through all the South Seas.[209] Nerval's Gérard chased after his lost Aurélia through all the heavens.[210] Turgenev's Arátoff, having dreamed he was dead beside dead Clara Militch, felt himself in her power until he perished in fevered bliss at the thought of rejoining her.[211] A Barrès heroine locked up in a morose cult of a dead lover offset a Barrès hero nurtured by the live memory of one.[212] Pascoli was dying to clasp a dead love to his bosom, if only to lament her absence.[213] A D'Annunzio heroine was mired in the memory of having held her dead lover in her arms a whole night long.[214] A bereaved lover in Rilke felt out with his feet the land of the dead for his sweetheart.[215] William Holman Hunt and John

White Alexander each painted Keats's Isabella brooding over a pot of basil containing her murdered lover's head.[216]

Love could follow in death's wake. "When she died he seemed to love for the first time," observed Bonaventura of a wife murderer, adding low-key: "Quietly he wedded Ines again."[217] Heine's statue-kissing boy grew up to fall in love with a girl seven years dead.[218] Berenice and Eleonora first aroused Poe's narrators in dying, and Poe's mystical Morella admonished her husband: "her whom in life thou didst abhor, in death thou shalt adore."[219] In Theodor Storm a seducer professed for a girl a passion that then turned real when she died: "for years now he has been carrying her fresh image around with him and is obliged to love a dead girl."[220] A Henry James hero, drawn into a couple's cult of their dead daughter, lived out an imaginary marriage with her topped off by her death.[221] And Turgenev's Arátoff told Clara Militch's ghostly presence: "After your death I fell passionately, irresistibly in love with you."[222]

Or love could wish its object dead, a wish commonly cast as a dream. Rousseau's Saint-Preux dreamed of his Julie as dead.[223] In Jean Paul a lover dreamed of his beloved with heart and forehead sunlit, lips and cheeks moonlit, face and hands moist, then realized: "You are dead, and your face has been oiled to make a death mask."[224] Heine dreamed of a sweet darling as dead,[225] and Berlioz orchestrated a love-sick composer's opium dream of murdering his sweetheart.[226] More common was the fantasy of loving to death. Sade's creatures might kill their sex partners in the act. Lewis's monk murdered the sister he raped.[227] In a Zacharias Werner drama Attila's bride thirsted lethally for Attila's blood on their wedding night.[228] In Kleist's stage shocker *Penthesilea* the Amazon queen and Achilles tore at each other's flesh until she kissed him to death.[229] Fouqué's soulless nymph Undine followed Penthesilea's lead with her trembling knight.[230] So did an overeager bride and groom in a poem by Justinus Kerner.[231] To take the guilty lovers in an Adolf Müllner drama at their fond word, he stripped her of her flesh like a lusty beast of prey while she stabbed him and sucked out his life's blood in her embrace.[232] Other romantic heroines such as Eichendorff's Romana or Stendhal's Mathilde[233] craved love and blood by quick turns. In both Pushkin and Gautier, Cleopatra put a new lover to death every morning.[234] Browning strangled his Porphyria in verse, whereupon "her cheek once more / Blushed bright beneath my burning kiss."[235] In Lermontov a fallen angel cornered his mortal love in a convent to kiss her dead.[236] Baudelaire poetized a girl's corpse decapitated by her lover.[237] "I would my love could kill thee": thus Swinburne.[238] Tennyson's Lucretius dreamed out a conflicted lust to mate and to slay, then in self-loathing "drove the knife into his side."[239] In Barbey d'Aurevilly a mute daughter of the house sneaked into a lodger's bed only to die in his arms.[240] A D'Annunzio hero murdered his sensual mistress in hopes of spiritualizing her.[241] Zola's human beast did likewise out of an atavistic urge to clinch his possession.[242] A prince hugged his princess to death (then disemboweled her pregnant corpse) in a Remy de Gourmont.[243] To convey death was the sacred feminine principle for Pierre Louÿs's temple prostitutes of old Alexandria.[244] Aubrey Beardsley penned a ballad of a barber who, smitten with a little princess, slit her throat and slipped away "softly as a dream."[245] Oscar Wilde's gallows ballad followed with the refrain: "Each man kills the thing he loves."[246] Octave Mirbeau's woman in the raw, Clara, ran a garden of deadly tortures for sexy kicks.[247] Jean Lorrain's Monsieur de Phocas, having discovered his penchant for sex murder, set sail for Egypt to indulge it.[248] Albert von Keller painted Love as a woman triumphant beside a lover she has decapitated.[249] Kokoschka coupled love and murder orgiastically in his play and poster *Murderer, Hope of Women.*[250] Even staid Bourdelle sculpted tragedy ever so Freudianly as a fair female nude expiring at the tip of a weeping murderer's sword.[251]

With fantasies of loving to death went fantasies of being loved to death—now distinct, now intermixed. Heine sang to nixies: "Kiss the life from out my breast."[252] Baudelaire saw himself as a hanged man devoured by vultures on the isle of love.[253] Poetically Swinburne envisioned "Queen Venus . . . full of death" at his bedside.[254] Dramatically Swinburne's Chastebard, for love of Mary Stuart, courted death in her chamber.[255] Novelistically Swinburne's Bertie told his sister: "Oh, I should like you to tread me to death, darling!" and "it would be jolly to feel you killing me."[256] D'Annunzio, after long echoing Swinburne,[257] outdid him with an orgasmic martyrdom of Saint Sebastian in dramatic French lyrics.[258] Bliss for Jean Lahor were to drink of his love's pure eyes and sweet breasts and then die, "my soul all embalmed with you!"[259] Man fed himself whole to woman alias the leech in Maurice Rollinat.[260] Man à la Rollinat also implored a merely cackling succubus: "Oh come! my heart bled dry so craves you as I die!"[261] Octave Mirbeau's voracious Clara worked a lover up into a murderous rage, then taunted him with sweet calm: "Kill me, darling."[262] Edvard Munch painted the death of Marat as a boudoir scene with a naked Charlotte Corday standing full-front, dead-pan, like a hatchet lady on duty—which would make it a study in loving to death except that the shadowy castrated corpse on the blood-drenched bed behind her was Munch's own mustached likeness.[263]

Not only Wagner played up the love-death.[264] In Zacharias Werner a Samaritan queen jubilated: "Ha! He lives! I can kill him—perish loving with him!"[265] Vigny and Baudelaire each memorialized a double suicide by young lovers.[266] Heine versified one couple drowning together and another kissing and crying, laughing and singing, as they froze to death.[267] Berlioz's Lelio yearned to sink into a last sleep with his true love one autumn evening.[268] For young Tennyson, "'Twere joy, not fear, claspt hand-in-hand with thee, / To wait for death."[269] Poe's lovers in "The Assignation" took poison separately in unison.[270] Poe's Madeline Usher in her bloody shroud bore her brother to the floor as a corpse.[271] In Swinburne, when a judge under the Terror had his victims stripped and bound "bosom to bosom to drown," a rude laborer paired with a fine beauty jubilated: "I shall drown with her, laughing for love."[272] Jean Lahor yearned for "a great love" to culminate in joint death amidst "the silence of measureless solitudes."[273] Flaubert's Anthony scourged himself into a frenzy fantasizing his own martyrdom opposite martyred Ammon-aria: "Our pain would have mingled, our souls would have mixed."[274] Villiers de l'Isle-Adam's warrior queen Akëdysséril ordered a couple exe-cuted at their sexual climax; by her high priest's contriving they killed themselves instead to head off a sexual anticlimax.[275] Villiers's Axël and Sara, likewise disdaining to live out their love, took poison and went into a passionate embrace.[276] When a sorry virgin gave herself to her dying lover in Zola, her heart literally burst.[277] On D'Annunzio's stage an inces-tuous couple got the same axe on the same block—"and," D'Annunzio specified, "the two bloods form the same puddle."[278] Art kept pace, from Ludwig Schnorr von Carolsfeld's lovers hugging awkwardly in midair as they plunged to their death[279] to Max Klinger's lovers locked in post-mortem improprieties amidst a sea of darkness.[280] And grand opera rou-tinely doomed lovers, as in Verdi's *Aida*, or drenched the boards with their blood for a curtain-ringer, as in Puccini's *Tosca*.[281] Exquisitely un-Shakespearian was Verdi's Otello stabbing himself over his victim Desdemona to the tune of their earlier love duet.[282]

Not just colloquially (as from time immemorial) was love's fulfillment, or passion spent, likened to dying. Unamuno found a foretaste of death in the act of love, "that spilling of one's vital substance."[283] Jean Lahor called that same spilling "a death delicious and deep."[284] More decorously, a thousand roses "gave out, in return for the love-light, / Their odorous souls in an ecstatic death" when Poe met his Helen.[285] To Baudelaire, the lover in the act looked like "a dying man caressing his tomb."[286] Out of Bartolomeo da Venezia's painting of a young courtesan offering flowers Huysmans read the warning: "Watch out! . . . An orgasm passes over into a death rattle beside her."[287] In songs by Schumann a loving woman yearned to die in a dream at her lover's breast,[288] and young Tennyson's Fatima craving her man hoped to "die, dying clasp'd in his embrace."[289] "Our sighs go off to the tomb," ran a women's love refrain by Maurice Rollinat,[290] and young Pirandello rhapsodized: "it is good to die / When you reach the goal."[291] Verlaine celebrated whores' arms "fresh like tombs."[292] Albert Samain apostrophized Woman: "Your arms, arms deep and sweet like death!"[293] And Death spoke to a lover through Samain: "When you pressed your lips to hers, / Did you not feel infinity / Where anguish fierce and helpless stirs? / . . . Then it was my mouth you kissed."[294] Félicien Rops drew Saint Theresa with a skull pressed to her vagina,[295] and Max Beckmann painted a death scene like an aftermath of sex[296]—which, though, takes us back from "death-in-love" (Rossetti's term) to death *and* love, where we began.

This sampling of the love-death linkup in nineteenth-century high culture may as well stop here. Not that I have cited its main forms; rather, such classifying is self-defeating by now, since the intermixes mostly resist being categorized. It is hard enough to fit a Sardanapalus or a House of Usher under topic heads. But what rubric of macabre erotism will accommodate a canvas covered with Penelope's slain suitors?[297] Or another with naiads converging to coddle dead Icarus?[298] Or, in fiction, a bride who turns out to be a dead jilted sweetheart,[299] or an anatomist who dissects his wife's lovers,[300] or one perpetual mourner who courts another,[301] or an adulteress laying out a dead lover on her marriage bed to await her husband's return?[302] Ungeneralizable love-death hybrids are only half the

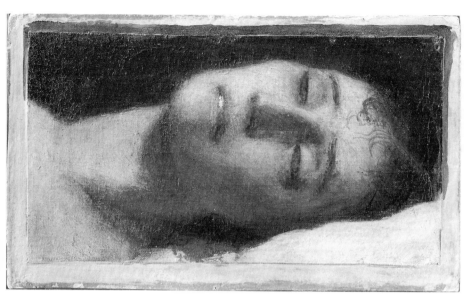

Figure 1. A study in death. Arnold Böcklin, *Dead Girl's Head*, 1879. (Öffentliche Kunstsammlung Basel, Kunstmuseum.)

Figure 2. Rejoining the elements. John Everett Millais, *Ophelia*, 1851–52. (Tate Gallery, London.)

Figure 3. In her element. Jean Delville, *Ophelia*, 1890. (Musées Royaux des Beaux-Arts, Brussels.)

Figure 4. A lyrical death. Jean Delville, *Orpheus*, 1893. (Anne-Marie Gillion Crowet, Brussels.)

Figure 5. Visiting her beloved. Homer Watson, *The Death of Elaine*, 1877. (Art Gallery of Ontario, Toronto.)

Figure 6. The best-loved corpse of the nineteenth century. Anne Louis Girodet de Roucy-Trioson, *Atala's Burial*, 1808. (Musée du Louvre, Paris.)

Figure 7. The seductive male corpse. Henry Wallis, *Chatterton*, 1855–56. (Tate Gallery, London.)

Figure 8. Deathlike for sex appeal. Eugène Delacroix, *Odalisque*, c. 1845–50. (Fitzwilliam Museum, University of Cambridge.)

Figure 9. Death's Venus. Romaine Brooks, *Le trajet*, c. 1911. (National Museum of American Art, Smithsonian Institution, Washington, D.C.)

Figure 10. Entrancing from beyond. Dante Gabriel Rossetti, *Beata Beatrix*, c. 1863. (Tate Gallery, London.)

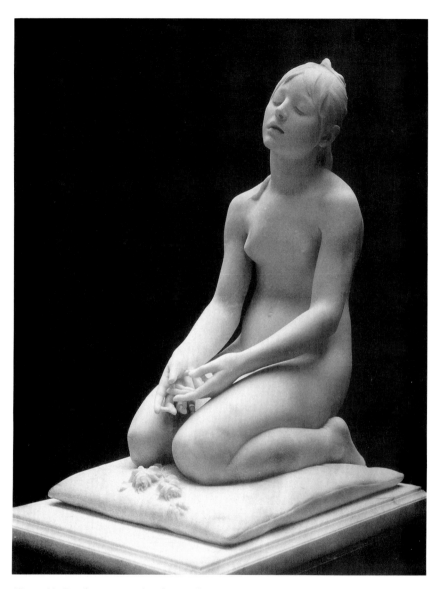

Figure 11. Death sweetened. Julien Dillens, *Figure for a Tomb*, 1885–87. (Musées Royaux des Beaux-Arts, Brussels.)

Figure 12. An Assyrian takes his treasures with him. Eugène Delacroix, *The Death of Sardanapalus*, 1827. (Musée du Louvre, Paris.)

Figure 13. Sardanapalus upstaged. Max Slevogt, *Sardanapalus*, 1907. (Niedersächsisches Landesmuseum, Hannover.)

Figure 14. An epidemic of fatal love. Gustave Moreau, *The Suitors*, 1852–98.
(Musée Gustave Moreau, Paris.)

Figure 15. Sex in extremis. Tony Robert-Fleury, *The Last Days of Corinth,* 1870. (Musée du Louvre, Paris.)

Figure 16. Lethally lovely. Edvard Munch, *Vampire*, 1895–1902. (Oslo Kommunes Kunstsamlingene, Munch-museet.)

Figure 17. The male corpse pursued. Pierre Paul Prud'hon, *Justice and Divine Vengeance Pursuing Crime*, 1815–18. (Musée du Louvre, Paris.)

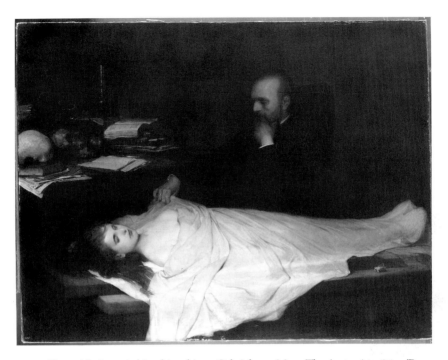

Figure 18. Approaching his subject. Gabriel von Max, *The Anatomist*, 1869. (Bayerische Staatsgemäldesammlungen, Munich.)

Figure 19. Love at a deathbed. Max Beckmann, *Big Death Scene*, 1905. (Bayerische Staatsgemäldesammlungen, Munich.)

Figure 20. Genteel infernal love. George Frederick Watts, *Paolo and Francesca*, 1872–84. (The Watts Gallery, Compton.)

Figure 21. Tortured infernal love. Gaetano Previati, *Paolo and Francesca*, 1901. (Galleria Civica d'Arte Moderna, Ferrara.)

Figure 22. LEFT: Full-blooded
spirits. Jean Delville, *Love of
Souls*, 1900. (Musée d'Ixelles,
Brussels.)
Figure 23. RIGHT: Sexily sink-
ing. Edward Burne-Jones, *The
Depths of the Sea*, 1887. (Fogg
Art Museum, Cambridge,
Massachusetts.)

Figure 24. Sex unto death. Max Klinger, *Finis*, 1881. (Kunsthalle Bremen.)

trouble at that; the other half is that the generalizable ones largely drew on traditional literary and artistic subjects to which the new century gave a new twist. Those subjects and that twist will be considered next, after one last nineteenth-century motif without much literary or artistic pre-history—the most overworked motif of the lot.

I mean the vampire motif, which flooded the nineteenth-century mar-ket for traffic with the dead. Folk belief in vampires battened in the Balkans on tidings of the bloodthirsty Wallachian prince Vlad IV and bloodthirstier Magyar countess Erzsébet Báthory, spreading to all of unlettered Europe by the late seventeenth century. Vampirism then pen-etrated polite literature as early as 1748[303] even while under fire from churchmen and philosophes alike. A half-century later Goethe himself gave it a high poetic licence with "The Bride of Corinth,"[304] and the lid blew.[305] Overnight, imperceptibly dead women began sucking blood—including female blood in Coleridge's *Christabel*, conceived as soon as Goethe's poem appeared in 1797. Byron broke the female monopoly in a few lines of *The Giaour* of 1813. But it was Byron's sometime compan-ion John William Polidori whose Lord Ruthven in *The Vampyre* of 1819 spawned the Byronic male breed of mysteriously seductive bloodsuckers that culminated in Bram Stoker's bisexual Dracula of 1897.[306] The female of the subspecies prevailed against even that potent breed. Such was her grip, or clutch, that Walter Pater saw the proud Mona Lisa herself as a vampire.[307] At the start of our century a thick-lipped, sinewy vamp was domesticated in the folksy form of dolls.[308] Vampires cast a scary yet irresistible spell; their victims were helplessly ensnared, entranced, sucked in, while their public thrilled wickedly. Vampirism spoke to the oral lust deep in us all, but the man-eating vamp was doubly sexy in that her bloodsucking also smacked of an unearthly thirst for sperm;[309] in a French pornographic classic she went after sperm outright.[310] Sex beyond the grave hinted at sex beyond the pale following the victim's swoon of surrender. Vampirism served a Baudelaire and a Munch to slur female sexuality.[311] It served Charlotte Brontë, Henry James, and Strindberg as a metaphor for women draining their men spiritually. Whatever its fig-urative uses—and there were lots more[312]—its bottom line remained the lascivious-lugubrious kiss of death.

These imaginings, then, and others like them, ran riot in the nine-teenth century. They spiced love with death, not, say, for Poe's aggrieved passenger who drowned himself with his wife's coffin—he would have preferred living on with his wife alive—but for Poe himself and, beyond Poe, for the vast readership that took pleasure in such imaginings. Though that pleasure might come as cold shivers, pleasure it decidedly was even then. And those imaginings were not just more abundant or more deeply felt than previous linkages of love and death. The difference was qualitative—and sharp. At least since Greco-Roman antiquity love and death had been seen as antithetical. To be sure, Christianity taught that death was for the blessed the start of a new life ruled by love—not, though, by the fleshly, earthly love at issue here: in the Christian hereafter, as far as churchly indications went, sex had been reserved to devils victimizing the wicked. But the post-Christian rapprochement between love and death is best grasped through the changed treatment of traditional subjects conspicuously coupling the two in the arts.

Three

Its Distinctiveness

From a juxtaposition of comparable premodern and modern works in the fine arts the distinctiveness of the nineteenth century's eroticization of death is often visible at a glance.

Death scenes abounded in premodern painting, with a premium on sightly nudes agonizing. Despite local exceptions such as the Dutch baroque or the Venetian rococo, fair flesh perished massively at the old masters' hands. But that flesh was fair differently, and perished differently, from its modern counterpart. Where the older art might flatter the dead and dying, the newer art sensualized them with the aid of deathliness itself. Such voluptuous casualties as Delacroix's Assyrian, Robert-Fleury's Corinthian, Rochegrosse's Babylonian, and Sartorio's Ephesian slave girls expiring bear the stamp of the 1800s. Nor did earlier beautified dead ever look much deader than merely limp or recumbent—as against Géricault's chalky capsized Hippolytus,[313] say, or William Etty's washed-out Leander,[314] or "the livid beauty of the female corpse in *Apollo Triumphant*" by Delacroix.[315] A death of Dido as seen by a Guercino, a Mattia Preti, or a Coypel was simply a dramatic misfortune.[316] But Millais's Ophelia belonged to her death: in her wet, florid tomb she was irresistibly in her element.[317] Even a morbid Rosso Fiorentino's Cleopatra met a dire fate in dying[318] where a Hans Makart's or a Jean François Gigoux's was luridly and alluringly fulfilled.[319] Martyrdoms in art had long been object lessons in suffering for the faith, female saints' pulchritude notwithstanding and even if their ecstatic transcendence of death, as in a Francesco del Cairo or a Guido Cagnacci, may look sexy to modern eyes.[320] The few nineteenth-century specimens were typically women martyred with no hint of who or why—mere bodies done to death.[321] Some eighteenth-century painters from Bencovich to Maulbertsch, Troger, and Fuseli frequently cast a deathly pallor over their figures. But the coquettish corpse in art dates from Jean Broc, Prud'hon, and Girodet in the nascent nineteenth century. Prud'hon's *Justice and Divine Vengeance Pursuing Crime*,[322] which David and Géricault both copied, alone spawned a whole run of softly gorgeous dead men.[323]

The death of lovers has long been a favorite in art, though its appeal has slowly declined over the centuries. No stylish medieval household was complete without an effigy of Pyramus and Thisbe or of Tristan and Isolt.[324] That Greek couple undone by a lion survived into the baroque. But the two medievals, trapped in a metaphysics of sorrow or an ethic of unfulfillment (as per Thomas d'Angleterre or Gottfried von Strassburg respectively), never even made it to the Renaissance; the romantics revived them, Wagner for a lusty double death. Two other medievals, Francesca and Paolo, slain as they slipped into sin, got through the Renaissance thanks to illustrations of Dante, who reported their posthumous fate: their surge of passion eternalized. Then in the nineteenth century they came into their own. Anselm Feuerbach painted them reading together;[325] Fuseli and Ingres, Delacroix and William Dyce, Lord Leighton and Arnold Böcklin, their mortal lapse;[326] Alexandre Cabanel, their look of passion in a dying embrace;[327] Rossetti, their transgression and its infernal sequel both.[328] But most rendered that sequel alone, and with mounting ardor from one to the next—William Blake, Ary Scheffer, Giuseppe Fraschieri, George Frederick Watts, Auguste Rodin, Arnold Böcklin again, Gaetano Previati, Umberto Boccioni.[329] Beginning with Fuseli's *Romeo at Juliet's Bier* of 1809, this other ill-starred couple got comparable pictorial play: Chassériau and Lord Leighton showed them embracing in death,[330] while Delacroix opted for Romeo lifting a bare-bosomed Juliet from her tomb.[331] The doomed lovers preferred by early moderns had been Hero and Leander, though with a focus on Leander; it took the nineteenth century for a drowning Leander to open his arms to his Hero.[332]

Figure 25. Sex for sinners hereafter. Taddeo di Bartolo, *Last Judgment,* c. 1393. (Collegiata di San Gimignano.)

Figure 26. Ecstasy of dying. Francesco del Cairo, *Saint Agnes*, 1635. (Galleria Sabauda, Turin.)

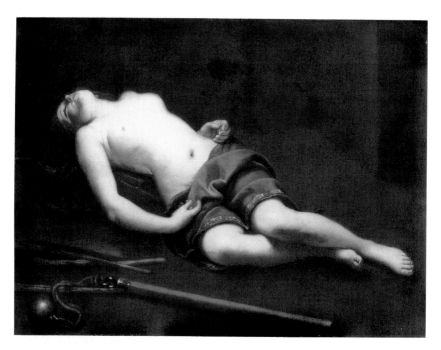

Figure 27. Ecstasy of death. Guido Cagnacci, *Young Martyr*, c. 1650. (Musée Fabre, Montpellier.)

Figure 28. Slain, yet none too dead. Swiss Master, *Cephalus and Procris*, c. 1530. (Öffentliche Kunstsammlung Basel, Kunstmuseum.)

Figure 29. Slain, yet none too dead either. Joachim Antonisz Wtewael, *The Death of Procris*, c. 1595. (The Saint Louis Art Museum.)

Figure 30. A dire fate. Giovanni Battista Rosso [Rosso Fiorentino], *The Death of Cleopatra*, c. 1528. (Herzog Anton Ulrich-Museum, Braunschweig.)

Figure 31. No love of death. Guido Reni, *The Death of Cleopatra*, c. 1628–30. (The Royal Collection, London.)

Figure 32. A dramatic misfortune. Mattia Preti, *The Death of Dido*, c. 1655. (Herzog Anton Ulrich-Museum, Braunschweig.)

Early moderns went in more for lovers just one of whom died. Venus and Adonis topped the lists, with Cephalus and Procris running a close second, Apollo and Hyacinth perhaps a distant third. The Venus and Adonis motif flourished above all in the high baroque, with Adonis never a convincing corpse and Venus, though perforce aphrodisiacal, only rarely coddling him dying—after a great Luca Cambiaso perhaps only in a Rubens drawing until the late eighteenth century.[333] Cephalus and Procris peaked in paint somewhat earlier—Cephalus rarely even tending his beloved prey, and Procris never managing to look moribund even with a protruding arrow or a gaping wound until (oddly) the formalism of a Canova or a Fabio Girardi around 1800.[334] As for Apollo and Hyacinth, artists celebrated only the god's gay love for the lad until, again at the very last, Benjamin West's Apollo of 1771, then Jean Broc's of 1801, tenderly supported his cherished, failing victim. The point of the deaths of lovers as depicted by premoderns was invariably that death destroyed love, period, with no redeeming grace or beauty, let alone erotic charm. Even as the turning came, the mythology changed: now a Criemhild fell all over a dead Siegfried.[335] Or else contemporary letters supplied new lovers' deaths: monkish Mélidor kissing a storm-drenched Phrosine who had caught her death rejoining him[336] or Celadon holding a glorious, ghostly Amelia struck by lightning.[337]

In a class apart were the mythological lovers most celebrated both earlier and later for their deaths: Orpheus and Eurydice. Of the Orpheus story it was Orpheus going after his Eurydice in Hades—the failed attempt to overcome death through love—that primarily claimed the old masters' attention. Some moderns too depicted this episode—Corot in a vast land-scape, Anselm Feuerbach in lugubrious grey on grey, Leighton with Orpheus fending off Eurydice's embrace, George Frederick Watts with Orpheus reaching for a deathlike Eurydice falling away from him.[338] Others showed Orpheus charming the beasts with his lyre, or else weeping beside Eurydice's corpse or atop her grave.[339] But most rendered his death in all its savage poetry: a ring of maenads closing in on him,[340] a nymph cradling his severed head on his lyre,[341] his head and lyre under water or in a landscape,[342] his lyre alone amid ghostly mourners in the moon-shine.[343] Pygmalion reversed the Orpheus myth but could not compete with it. In the old iconography his marble Galatea came to life sponta-neously; in the new he caressed her to life.[344] Zenobia out of Tacitus, stabbed and thrown into a stream by her husband to protect her from rape, resurfaced for a competition of 1850 as Bouguereau, Baudry, and Émile Lévy all painted Roman shepherds resuscitating the corpselike beauty.

At one premodern juncture corpses were depicted with a gruesome stress on rotting flesh: following the Black Death of 1348, in the so-called transi tombs and, beginning a century later, the popular woodcuts of northern Europe. After 1400 the same inspiration gave rise to the Dance of Death, "in essence a macabre parody of the dance of love,"[345] whereby one participant decked out as a decomposing corpse, later as a skeleton, led the others off in a frenzied two-step. A gradually stylized skeleton or "bone man" overran even Renaissance Italy, though spreading less terror there than elsewhere: by 1595 iconologist Cesare Ripa could prescribe instead a "bone woman" in flowing robes to symbolize death.[346] The French in their Renaissance renewed and upgraded the older lifelike (rather than deathlike) mortuary sculpture memorializing the deceased even as the Reformation and Counter-Reformation brought the transis to an end.[347] The skeleton, ordinarily male, persisted nonetheless in pictorial art as a grim token of death ahead and an intended damper on sensual delight. It held its lead as death symbol straight through the nineteenth century even while a counterimage arose of death as a voluptuous temptress, as in Gustave Moreau's *The Young Man and Death* of 1856–65. A variant derived from Flaubert's Saint Anthony tempted by a shrouded, wriggling female physique topped off by a death's head:[348] Odilon Redon replicated and Félicien Rops popularized this saintly vision.[349] In literature as against art, death as a seductress swept the field from Goethe on. That lethal lady coaxed a fisherman overboard in a Goethe ballad.[350] She played dice for the soul of Coleridge's Ancient Mariner and urged Chateaubriand's René in the wilderness to "mix fleshly joys with death."[351] Leopardi called her a "fairest maiden."[352] In Espronceda an old man dreamed of her coaxing him into her bed.[353] Whitman praised the universe for her "sure-enwinding arms."[354] She was a promise of peace to a distraught Rachilde hero,[355] and to a lover in Albert Samain she cooed: "Come to sweet Death, your longed-for love."[356] Even as a scary Rat Wife in Ibsen she could lure little Eyolf to the depths of the sea with beguiling talk of the dark and quiet there.[357] Almost alone in letters at the time, Thomas Mann's *Death in Venice* retained the seasoned bone man, indeed in three

Figure 33. Gay love dying. Jean Broc, *The Death of Hyacinth*, 1801. (Musée de la Ville de Poitiers et de la Société des Antiquaires de l'Ouest, Poitiers.)

Figure 34. Galatea comes to life. Jean Raoux, *Pygmalion*, 1717. (Musée Fabre, Montpellier.)

Figure 35. Pygmalion caresses Galatea to life. Jean Léon Gérôme, *Pygmalion and Galatea*, 1892. (The Metropolitan Museum of Art, New York.)

Figure 36. Close mourning. John Henry Fuseli [Johann Heinrich Füßli], *Criemhild Throwing Herself on Dead Siegfried*, 1817. (Kunsthaus Zurich.)

Figure 37. Death goes after sex. John Henry Fuseli [Johann Heinrich Füßli], *Sin Pursued by Death*, 1794–96. (Kunsthaus Zurich.)

Figure 38. LEFT: Embracing death. Edvard Munch, *Death and the Maiden*, 1894. (Oslo Kommunes Kunstsamlingene, Munch-museet.)
Figure 39. RIGHT: Unwelcome death. Hans Baldung Grien, *Death and the Young Woman*, 1517. (Öffentliche Kunstsammlung Basel, Kunstmuseum.)

Figure 40. LEFT: Easing death's way. Niklaus Manuel Deutsch, *Death as a Warrior Embraces a Young Woman*, 1517. (Öffentliche Kunstsammlung Basel, Kunstmuseum.)

Figure 41. RIGHT: Welcome into death. Pierre Eugène Émile Hébert, *Et toujours! Et jamais!*, 1859–63. (Spencer Museum of Art, University of Kansas, Lawrence.)

Figure 42. At peace with her death. Antoine Wiertz, *La belle Rosine*, 1847. (Musée Wiertz, Brussels.)

Figure 43. "... mêlons des voluptés à la mort!" Gustave Moreau, *The Young Man and Death*, 1856–65. (Fogg Art Museum, Cambridge, Massachusetts.)

Figure 44. LEFT: An orgy of lust and carnage. Oskar Kokoschka, "Kokoschka: Drama-Komödie": poster for *Mörder, Hoffnung der Frauen* (*Murderer, Hope of Women*), 1909. (The Museum of Modern Art, New York.)

Figure 45. RIGHT: Grim sex. Heinrich Davringhausen, *The Sex Murderer*, 1917. (Bayerische Staatsgemäldesammlungen, Munich.)

Figure 46. Bosomy death. Odilon Redon, *Death: My Irony Exceeds All Others!*, 1889. (Kunstmuseum, Winterthur.)

Figure 47. Death and the maiden updated. Hans Ruedi Giger, *Li II*, 1974. (Property of the artist.)

Figure 48. Timeless love. Michael Zulli, *Taboo* No. 5, 1991.

successive apparitions—repellent as in his heyday, yet fascinating enough even so to ensnare the austere, inward hero.[358]

An offshoot of the Dance of Death was the theme of Death and the Maiden, which likewise originated in Germany and flourished during the Reformation.[359] Its adepts—Hans Baldung Grien, Niklaus Manuel Deutsch, Barthel Beham—never tired of depicting succulent female flesh at the mercy of a hideous grinning bone man. The message was graphic: that death had the last, grim word against fleshly delights. Nowhere was the contrast between erotism personified and death personified more pointed. This folk theme overran Europe, penetrating even the elitist cultures of France and Italy. In a German folk song of the late sixteenth century, "Es ging ein Mägdlein zarte," the Maiden shuddered as Death's voice sounded through her window. Matthias Claudius reworked this text in 1775 as if to mark the incipient change in sensibility toward death: now the Maiden ceased shuddering as the bone man wooed her with fond words. Schubert struck this new note in his haunting song and quartet of 1824 based on the Claudius rewrite, then again in "The Fisher Maiden" of 1828 using a Heine ballad.[360] Mussorgski reworked a collaborator's text in this same vein for the "Serenade" of 1875 in his *Songs and Dances of Death*. Munch gave the new view of death as tempter its sharpest contours in an etching of 1894 showing the bone man and a naked beauty locked in a hot embrace.[361] The old view had spilled over in its time into many a vanitas picturing a beautiful woman, often mirroring herself, with an unobserved skull or skeleton nearby. In the great modern vanitas, *La belle Rosine* of 1847 by Antoine Wiertz, a resplendent woman instead looked the skeleton in the eyes, smiling serenely. In the mid–seventeenth century Calderón and Andreas Gryphius each put on stage a lover who found himself embracing a skeleton in place of his beloved: lust for the flesh was an ephemeral mistake.[362] This same misadventure later befell many a romantic character, only without conveying that simple lesson. Repeatedly in Jan Potocki's picaresque *The Manuscript Found in Zaragoza* of 1803–15 the hero's women turned into corpses, even two at a time. So did loved ones in Heine's verses. Like one bride in Heine,[363] Espronceda's philandering student of Salamanca suffered this undeceiving once and for all.[364] A popular variant was the French girl of one night with a ribbon around her neck who turned out to have been guillotined: she went from Thomas Moore to Horace Smith to Washington Irving to Pétrus Borel to Alexandre Dumas.[365] In a spooky-spoofy Gogol a seminarist dreamed he killed an old witch haunting him, who then turned into a beautiful girl: he woke back up to a death watch of an old hag and died of fright.[366] From one such grisly tall tale to the next, the effect was to take the cold edge off the erotic encounter with death.

A figure close to the seductress symbolizing death shaped up along with her: the femme fatale. If the siren is at least as old as Odysseus, the stereotypical siren was a period piece produced in bulk in the late nineteenth century. For all her diverse romantic forerunners,[367] her prototypes were chiefly two: Swinburne's feminine ideal in poetry[368] and Rossetti's in paint.[369] Aloof, self-absorbed, coldly handsome, she was content to watch men destroy themselves loving her. A parallel French breed was more enterprising. Villiers de l'Isle-Adam's Isis already obliterated a lover through sensual surfeit.[370] Her successors used sharper weapons, often unspecified, among them Jean Lorrain's glaucous-eyed Lorelei exuding "the philtre of death."[371] By the Yellow Nineties that clichéd demoness was accumulating enthralled victims all over in Western letters, with her Anglo-French extraction showing even in Italy despite D'Annunzio's extravagant cult of her,[372] and especially in Germany[373] short of Wedekind's devastating Lulu. Painting kept pace with letters: witness Edward Burne-Jones's demonic deep-sea mermaid,[374] Gustave Moreau's lurid bride of the night,[375] Fernand Khnopff's predatory panther lady,[376] or János Vaszary's Munchlike monster of gorgeousness with blood-red hair.[377] The femme fatale, however garishly styled, tended to stand for woman as such, as in Jean Lahor's plaint to Dalilah: "How, woman, . . . thou who givest life, art thou full of death?"[378]—or in Stuck's figure of Sin wrapped in Eve's serpent as a sexy shawl.[379] After the turn of the century the cliché dissolved into far-flung derivatives—Hanns Heinz Ewers's spider woman weaving at a window whose hands hypnotized male neighbors into hanging themselves,[380] or Bruno Frank's silent-movie vamp from whose lips a mesmerized spectator read love messages to himself.[381] Bruno Frank's star of "The Vampire" incidentally illustrates the overlap of female vampires with femmes fatales, and of both with the fantasy of being loved to death. So does Munch's unholy Madonna with her halo of blood (and "smile of a corpse")[382] or Hanns Heinz Ewers's Alraune literally draining men's hearts.[383]

The supreme femmes fatales were two traditional figures updated: Salome foremost, with Judith bringing up the rear. The biblical Judith won the favor of Holofernes, an enemy commander besieging her city, only to lop off his head with his sword as he slept and carry it home in triumph. Premodern Judiths in art were proud killers shown committing that loveless deed with unladylike ferocity or else packing up and off afterwards with no tender heed for their bloody booty.[384] Here was no eroticized death, but death as the punitive price of a Judith often overwhelmingly sexy.[385] Hebbel's stageplay *Judith* of 1840 introduced a new Judith whose divine calling to save her people was only her coverup of a conflicted love for a macho Holofernes. Thus modernized, Judith fast became a bloody heroine of the one-sided love-death in art. Max Liebermann painted her in mortal erotic combat with Holofernes, Klimt her evil thrill while petting the severed head, Max Slevogt her picture on his easel with a sword drawn on him.[386] Klimt's Judith was of a perverse kind with his Salome.[387] Far more popular than Judith by and large, Salome also underwent a more radical metamorphosis over the centuries. Medievals showed her as a decorous, demure little dancer at Herod's feast and a dutiful daughter fetching the head of her mother's detractor, John the Baptist, at her mother's bidding. In the Renaissance she was graduated to a disquieting young beauty with a knowing complicity in evil even as she remained chillingly impassive toward the head she received or bore on a charger. By way of contrast her mother, Herodias, was wont to snatch that head up eagerly, often mutilating the tongue with manic glee. The mother's exhilaration only mounted in the Baroque,[388] though then the main action shifted to the beheading, with Salome's gaze usually averted and often pensive or downright doleful.[389] Fuseli lent the subject an enigmatic new suggestiveness toward 1800 with mother, daughter, and maid all lithe and luscious in sheer, shimmering gauze as if in some enchanted palace of delights except for the daughter's trayload.[390] But as with Judith, the decisive renewal again came from literature, in this case from Heine's romantic swan song of 1847, *Atta Troll*, which rhymed a folk tradition about Herodias hankering after an unresponsive John whose head she demanded in a fit of pique only to die kissing it, crazed with grief. Following Heine, writers from Flaubert to Wilde, artists from Moreau to Picasso, composers from Massenet to Strauss competed to

render Herodias and soon Salome in increasingly overcharged erotic traffic with the Baptist or more frequently with his hapless head alone.[391] By
the early 1900s "the macabre maiden," as Henry James called her,[392] was
preeminently the darling of the cultural élite. Fabled lady-killers there
were too who caught the public fancy, but no blood-and-guts homme
fatal of a Salome's standing. Don Juan hardly figured, even counting
Byron's ingénu.[393] Perseus and the Medusa's head never got much beyond
Cellini's statue of 1545–54.[394] And David, after a promising playful debut
with his foot on Goliath's head in Donatello's statue of about 1430, drew
no closer than that to his grisly trophy except once to hold it in his lap
in a juvenile Tiepolo.[395]

For all that, love was happily paired with death before modern times
in depictions of one venerable subject: Mary Magdalen. Nominally this
sometime sinner stood for the vanity of fleshly indulgence, which she
renounced to follow Jesus. But she was also by tradition the betrothed of
Christ, their nuptials to be celebrated on high. Perhaps this is why she
enjoyed the unique iconographical privilege of ascending to heaven stark
naked.[396] Paul had declared heaven sex-free—which was hard to square
with the resurrection of the flesh, but which premodern artists honored
by deft figleafery, with this single, shocking exception. Back on earth the
Magdalen attended Jesus in anguish beside his mother at his death and
burial,[397] and Jesus appeared to her first on his way back to heaven. By
herself she presented originally as a passionate penitent overcoming
worldly vanity—scraggly, wasted, hideous—or else in modest devotion
beside a crucifix, a skull, and (having annointed the Savior's feet) an oil
jug. But by the sixteenth century the bride-to-be in pious retreat was
more often to be seen as a voluptuous nude fondling a death's head and
gazing longingly aloft. A baroque Jesuit put it that "she burned with such
love for the Lord that she could not endure her clothing."[398] Probably
the foremost celebrant of her deathward erotic thrust was a seventeenth-
century Florentine priest, Francesco Furini, but the competition was
stiff.[399] All her high erotic investment in death notwithstanding, the Magdalen hardly flourished in the nineteenth century. Her old lines of rep-
resentation fell away with Christianity itself; her best late showings in
them were a crucifixion by Gaetano Previati with the other two Marys
bearing her up, a lamentation by Böcklin with her wailing unattended,
and a few pious pinups.[400] Hebbel's domestic drama *Maria Magdalene* of

Figure 49. Bringing her booty home. Hans Baldung Grien, *Judith*, 1525. (Germanisches Nationalmuseum, Nuremberg.)

Figure 50. The loveless deed. Lucas Cranach the Elder, *Judith with the Head of Holofernes*, c. 1530. (Národni Galerie, Prague.)

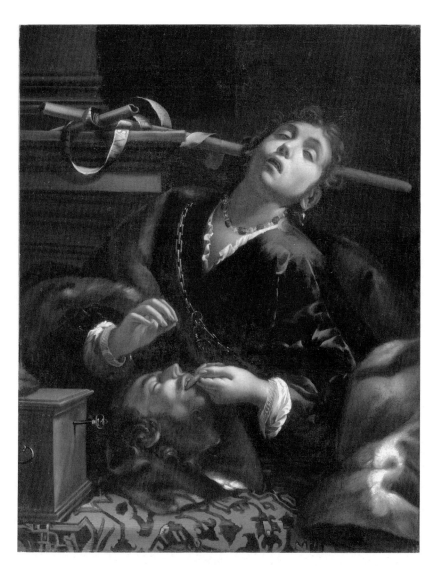

Figure 51. Baroque morbidity. Francesco del Cairo, *Herodias with the Head of Saint John the Baptist*, 1650. (Museum of Fine Arts, Boston.)

Figure 52. The none too gentle touch. Peter Paul Rubens, *Judith*, c. 1606–7. (Herzog Anton Ulrich-Museum, Braunschweig.)

Figure 53. Perfectly aloof. Niklaus Manuel Deutsch, *Salome with the Head of Saint John the Baptist*, c. 1518. (Öffentliche Kunstsammlung Basel, Kupferstichkabinett.)

Figure 54. LEFT: Flirting. Franz von Stuck, *Salome*, 1906. (Städtische Galerie im Lenbachhaus, Munich.)
Figure 55. RIGHT: A grisly foible. Gustav Klimt, *Judith I*, 1901. (Národni Galerie, Prague.)

Figure 56. Salome unveiled. Pablo Picasso, *Salome*, 1905. (Sprengel Museum, Hannover.)

1843 failed to update her, its only real connection with her being her misspelled surname in the title. Wilkie Collins only travestied her in *The New Magdalen*, a novel and play of 1873 about a sometime prostitute who swiped a seemingly dead lady's identity to go respectable. Paul Heyse in *Maria of Magdala* of 1907, then Maurice Maeterlinck in *Mary Magdalen* of 1908, returned her to Jerusalem, but only for her to squirm over a Roman's offer to save Jesus in return for her favors. Baudelaire likened his sick taste for a sickly whore to her ardor for Jesus: "I lick her silently with greater heat / Than Mary Magdalen the Savior's feet."[401] Rossetti composed a sonnet to match his drawing of her running from a clinging escort to Jesus: "He needs me, calls me, loves me: let me go!"[402] Félicien Rops etched her as a whore hugging the feet of a bleeding, sneering Christ crucified on a stained-glass window with the Moulin Rouge for a halo.[403] Rodin sculpted and Lovis Corinth painted her none too differently, her naked body pressed halfway up a Jesus halfway down from the cross.[404] She could be brought no closer than that to necrophilia, if even that close, without becoming unrecognizable. As against Judith and Salome, and despite her emblematic death's head, she was a figure of full-blooded life eternal—of carnality postponed. By nineteenth-century standards her erotic vocation for death was misleading.

And what of her holy bridegroom? He too had no love of dead bodies: he preached the resurrection. On the other hand, the rituals and imagery of Christianity centered in his corpse. He had suffered mortally for us all at the last. His torn flesh and spilt blood were the holiest of the holy. The Christian communion reenacted his sacrifice. Christian prayers and oaths alike invoked his wounds. Christian iconography featured the crucifixion, the descent from the cross, the lamentation, the pietà, the entombment. In these alone would premodern artists ever depict a corpse naturalistically; indeed, they commonly accentuated its corpselikeness beyond the natural from the fourteenth century on. If corpses were drawn from nature as early as the 1430s,[405] Christ's alone got the touch of death in paint. Its coloration was frequently an eerie olive, sometimes a ghostly white, occasionally red, purple, blue, brown, or yellow.[406] Often it appeared contorted or shriveled with pain on the cross and after, its raw wounds crying out. Beginning in the late Renaissance the mood blackened as if competitively from one master to the next—sepulchral in Giovanni Bellini, Cosmè Tura, and Mantegna,[407] poignant-grisly in the Master of Saint Bartholomew and Rosso Fiorentino,[408] in Grünewald and Amico Aspertini,[409] in Holbein and Hans Baldung Grien,[410] even in Correggio and Bronzino,[411] macabre in Girolamo Romanino and Morales,[412] ghastly in Annibale Carracci, Gregorio Fernández, Alessandro Turchi.[413] A few eroticized the pietà, Michelangelo foremost.[414] Some feminized dead Jesus a little; a rococo virtuoso in marble actually prettified him under a diaphanous shroud.[415] But the norm was a man of deepest spirituality desexualized, devastated, weighed down with immeasurable sorrow in dying. Such a Christ demanded of worshippers a passion for his drastically dead body well beyond whatever morbid propensities they may have brought with them to the altar. To be a Christian was to embrace that broken remnant of humankind in one's heart; to kiss its wounds in one's heart was saintliness pure. Catherine of Siena having drunk the pus from an old lady's sores in 1375, Christ appeared to her with his juiciest gashes oozing and whispered: "Drink, daughter, the fluid from my side," whereupon she "put her body's, but even more her soul's, lips to the holiest wound and eagerly drank long and deep of that indescribable, unfathomable fluid."[416] And around 1750 Ludwig von Zinzendorf, who led the Moravian Brethren, preached that we should all "like to kiss ourselves dead" on the dead Christ's "wound-sweetness" and "to lie with his corpse a whole eternity," the blessed few being those "whom the bloody mouth has kissed, whom the corpse of Jesus has embraced, on whom that corpse has stretched out limb to limb, whom it has known."[417]

Dead Christs dwindled in northern art after the Reformation, then throughout Europe as the faith waned. At the same time the old images in the old churches lost their force of reality for residual believers; like the gospels themselves, they ceased being taken at face value. Most made their way into museums. The few credible modern imitations—by Prud'hon, Flandrin, Delacroix, Trübner, Böcklin, Stuck, Rouault, Henner[418]—followed faster. Attempts by the Nazarenes or the Pre-Raphaelites in the nineteenth century to revive the old devotional art only pointed up its pastness. The love once given dead Jesus found other, unholy outlets. Often it showed its origin outright. Sex went mortuary in Christ's name when Chateaubriand's Amélie declared herself to René in her Carmelite coffin.[419] Sacrilege well beyond Chateaubriand's brought the underpinnings of the old adoration of Christ into the open. The old adoration of the Virgin led the way: her image was a first temptation for

Lewis's monk and Flaubert's Anthony[420] before becoming a lewd obsession in a Mirbeau, a Gourmont, a Huysmans.[421] A libertine priest in
another Mirbeau would see from the foot of the crucifix "Christ's body
sway on bloody nails, come loose, tip over, fall away, and in place of this
vanished God: triumphant Woman, stark naked, the eternal prostitute
offering her mouth, her genitals, thrusting out her whole body for vile
kisses"[422]—a substitution graphic in Félicien Rops.[423] And a gay priest of
Mirbeau's would daydream of the crucified Christ after the fashion of a
latter-day Catherine of Siena or Ludwig von Zinzendorf: "To run one's
repentent lips over that adorable body, to press one's mouth against the
gaping wounds in those aching thighs, to kiss those broken limbs, to feel
that heavenly flesh burn against one's mortal flesh!"[424] In Gourmont a
blasphemous couple aligned their caresses with Christ's agony, replicating
by turns "the kiss of the thorns, the touch of the leaded lashes, the cherished bite of the nails, the carnal penetration of the lance, the spasms of
death, the joys of decay."[425] At a mixed sodomite black mass in Huysmans
the women masturbated around a phallic crucifix.[426] Jean Lorrain imag-
ined a fleshy pagan androgyne beneath the Christ of a classic Descent
from the Cross.[427] Norman Lindsay painted a triumphant bacchanal
before a wasted, desolate Christ expiring.[428] A German graveyard vampire
celebrated an orgiastic victory over Christ in an emancipated nunnery.[429]
Oskar Kokoschka's *Pietà* poster of 1908 with its interlaced chalk-faced
Madonna and red, naked Jesus came close to illustrating Rilke's "Pietà"
of 1906: "We never lay together earlier, / . . . / How strange we both
should go to ruin now."[430] Such eroticization of Christ's death, latent in
the old pieties, now spilled over into the century's sexed-up corpses and
terminal ecstasies at large. A moronic old shepherd in a German story
drew the one connection as he went mad for a dead girl he stumbled
upon: she reminded him of a Christ child buried in his boyhood mem-
ories of church.[431] As for those terminal ecstasies, was not deadly sex in
person, the femme fatale, the ascetical Savior in simple reverse?

The love once given dead Jesus found other, unholy outlets: this process attended, but did not cause, the reconciliation of love with death in
the arts. That reconciliation began around 1775 and progressed quite
steadily with a final, sharp upswing around 1900. Its bottom line was a
protest against death, one that was by no means exclusively erotic but
that did fix on erotism by predilection. This fixing began rather like a

nightmare with "Lenore," Fuseli, *The Monk*, "The Bride of Corinth," Bonaventura, *The Vampyre*, "La Belle Dame Sans Merci," the *Symphonie Fantastique*. Though the romantics and then especially the decadents routinized it, the mythicization of sex in the crypt retained a pathological edge and dampened shock effect to the last. More, it was strained, contrived, less than sincere, like a dubious struggle to accept the unacceptable: death. What brought on that struggle?

What brought it on was Christ's afterworld falling away along with Christianity itself. By the end of the eighteenth century Christianity was no longer simple fact even for those who remained Christian. Panic sounded through pious Jean Paul's ironic fantasy of Christ breaking it to the dead at their gravesides that the universe was godless.[432] The stakes in the hereafter were erotic for Goethe's young Werther and Ugo Foscolo's Jacopo Ortiz dying lovesick, likewise for Novalis at his sweetheart's grave.[433] Christ's collapsed eternity showed in, or through, many a vision of carnal love beyond death. Heine was sweetly jocular about it: when other corpses rose for the Last Judgment he and his love would lie behind together.[434] Thomas Lovell Beddoes was tragical: in his *Death's Jest Book* a duke had his wife's grave dug out that he might join her in earth rather than heaven, for "I loved no desolate soul" but "those lovely limbs, those tender members."[435] Villiers de l'Isle-Adam was sententious in "Véra," with its posthumous sex: "Death is definitive only for those who have hopes of heaven."[436] A visual counterpart was Jean Delville's *Love of Souls*, with its lovers' distinctly bodily embrace.[437]

Post-Christian lovers denying death had their moments of truth. For all his hopes of love after death, fictitious Élie Mariaker could not overwrite his glimpse of the void ("I sounded out a corpse, a hand upon its heart").[438] A Turgenev narrator flew by night with an enchantress who drained his blood until a ghastly yellowish-black cloud suddenly loomed upon them; he woke up in panic as she who had thought to cheat death vanished, crying: "Annihilation! Annihilation!"[439] Most tormented was Maupassant. In one of his tales a raconteur scoffed bitterly at "those crosses and marble slabs where a dead man's relatives post their regrets, their wishes for his happiness in the next world, their hopes of rejoining him: jokers!"[440] And in another a lover caught digging up his mistress's corpse explained himself in the courtroom: "She is *dead*. Do you understand this word? Never, never, never, anywhere, will this being exist any more."[441]

It is of fundamental importance that on the whole the modern linkup of love with death was sheer fantasy play. Some actualizing there was, by cultural figures and by society at large, but none demonstrably in excess of the usual quota of morbid antics for any age. In this Flaubert spoke for his century: "I have dreamed, but acted little."[442] Of the cultured set, Kleist notably acted out, indeed all-out: turned on by dying women, he found one to join him in suicide. Zacharias Werner declared darkly that he alone understood "The Bride of Corinth," for "death enfolded me in bands of love."[443] Heine avowed on his deathbed that he had loved only statues and corpses.[444] Beddoes and Nerval wound up as suicides, though for no known erotic reason. Rossetti had his Beata Beatrix (Elizabeth Siddal) exhumed ceremonially by moonlight in 1869 to recover the love poems he had buried with her seven years before. Alfred Gilbert sculpted a sepulcher to hold a doctor's ashes together with, later, the doctor's widow's and then—as he fell for the widow—his own.[445] When corpse-likeness was sexy in the decadent days, Sarah Bernhardt was photographed asleep in a coffin and Ida Rubinstein was painted as an anorexic Aphrodite.[446] Renée Vivien went one better and starved herself to death at thirty-two (not without first converting to Catholicism).[447] In correspondence, Clemens Brentano bade Caroline von Günderode open her veins for him to drink himself drunk on her blood while bemoaning her death, only to add on second thought: "Don't open your veins, Günderödchen, I'll bite them open."[448] More delicately, Keats told his beloved Fanny: "I have two luxuries to brood over in my walks, your loveliness and the hour of my death. O that I could have the possession of them both in the same minute."[449] Oscar Wilde put it sententiously to his Bozie: "Death and love seem to walk on either hand as I go through life."[450] Flaubert cherished the blended memory of lemon trees and rotting corpses in Jaffa—"the great synthesis."[451] Maurice Barrès in his journal gushed over Spanish churches with their bloody crucifixions and putrescent odors, noting: "But above all, what did I love so much in Venice, Toledo, Sparta, what drew me towards Persia? Cemeteries."[452] Berlioz in his diary claimed to have been so taken with a dead woman in a passing hearse in Florence that "I would have kissed her had I been alone."[453] The Goncourt brothers in their diary related after visiting a women's hospital that the memory of the pale sufferers in white sheets aroused them sexually—which puzzled them inasmuch as they found the likes of the Marquis de Sade "nauseating."[454] And so on down to triviality. Sade himself, for all his "infamies" as he himself called them, had no truck with corpses as far as the records disclose.

Society at large acted out still less on balance. Queen Victoria mourned her Prince Consort with exemplary excess. France's bout of *boulangisme* ended with Boulanger's suicide on his mistress's grave. The necrophiliac milestone was Mayerling in 1889 by dint of the impassioned public curiosity it aroused: there Crown Prince Rudolf of Habsburg killed a love-and-death partner and, long hours later, himself beside her.[455] Crown Prince Rudolf's closest rival in kind was Sergeant Bertrand, a confessed French necrophile who achieved legendary standing at midcentury; yet Bertrand's exploits, probably apocryphal,[456] pale beside those of Gilles de Rais four centuries earlier, which Stendhal discovered and Huysmans publicized.[457] Jack the Ripper, who terrorized fin-de-siècle female London, was no match for that Magyar guzzler of female blood Erzsébet Báthory, nor did he likely titillate his victims as he did newspaper readers throughout the West. What was new was not such deathly sexy doings, but the press they got—of all descriptions. Anecdotes about necrophilia filled the memoirs of the times.[458] Learned treatises on it proliferated around 1900.[459] Monographs on vice featured mortuary chambers in brothels.[460] Another standby, prostitution in cemeteries, went back to antiquity. So did necrophilia among priests, embalmers, and gravediggers. If the morgue was popular with Parisian strollers in the nineteenth century, so in the fifteenth century was the charnel house in the churchyard of the Innocents.

Necrophilia in action is hard to quantify because it mostly goes undetected and because important detected varieties such as murder-then-rape go uncounted. Officially it was not reported at all in Great Britain and the United States, or by itself anywhere, during the period at issue. On the European continent it was lumped together with other misdeeds in criminal statistics—desecration of tombs and their appurtenances in France, offenses against religion in Italy, these plus disturbing the peace of the dead in the Germanies. Austria-Hungary probably came closest to reporting necrophilia alone, under the head of unauthorized opening or damaging of graves or tampering with corpses; increasingly intricate breakdowns of offenses and offenders according to ever-more-numerous variables left the Danubian tabulations ten years behindhand by the time the Dual Monarchy crumbled in 1918. Systematic yearly accounting under those all-too-broad rubrics dated from 1830 in France, 1863 in Austria-Hungary, 1865 in Baden, 1875 in Italy, 1883 in Bavaria. If the share of necrophilia in the various totals remained however roughly constant over the years (the only reasonable assumption), the one clear indication is negative across the board: nowhere did necrophilia in practice rise or fall significantly while it soared crescendolike in creative works in the decades around 1900. In other words, fact and fancy were unrelated. Besides, clinical researchers on necrophiliac criminality concurred at the time that the typical offenders were mental defectives—hardly the readership of a Heine or a Leopardi, a Poe or a Baudelaire.

Fantasy was at variance with reality also in that even while death was being highlighted in fantasy it was being covered up or pushed aside in actual human arrangements.[461] In the nineteenth century the sight of the dead, formerly a common, ritualized experience, turned terrifying even as death turned definitive. The propped-up mummies in an old Capucin cemetery outside Palermo could still amuse a Dumas somewhat nervously in 1836, where in 1885 they traumatized a Maupassant.[462] Eroticized death bridged in the mind the newly absolute, and petrifying, divide between life and death. Hence its imagery was protectively abstract, hazy, immaterial; or else it confined itself to fresh corpses or, alternatively, deathless corpses out of folklore. Hence too it might be as frightful as it was wishful. It might also collapse into reality the way a dream sometimes collapses into a nightmare: witness the recurrent theme of the disconsolate lover who, as in Dumas fils or Maupassant, digs up a beloved's corpse only to sicken from the sight and smell of it.[463] Some, including Georg Heym, could not make believe erotically about death: "Are you what once I ardently embraced?" Heym asked a corpse he then fled.[464] Least of all could Maurice Rollinat, whose obsession with cherished flesh rotting took him into the madhouse.[465] The love-death mix might, finally, project its own nightmare onto reality, as in the sudden syphilis scare of those decadent decades (graphic in the *Mors syphilitica* of Félicien Rops)[466] when the disease had long since plateaued.[467] This decadent fantasy of syphilis rampant threw back to the Christian fantasy of death as the wages of sin. Indeed, it is not hard to recognize in the new postmortem illusion of eroticized death the old postmortem illusion revamped. Christ's message of conquering death through love is legible beneath the nineteenth century's flirtation with death. Sex after death in this world was Christian with a new twist. Its derivation from the shambles of Christianity is the easier to see in that both were purely ideational, pure mental constructs, their contacts with reality only peripheral and problematic.

But was love for or among the dead so very new in Western letters? Petrarch comes to mind, craving his Laura in and beyond death. "Oh grasping earth, how I do envy you / Embracing her I may no longer see":[468] just these lines, taken in isolation, might give pause—wrongly, for by that earth's embrace Petrarch meant above all a screening from sight, as emerges from the sequel: "And hiding that fair countenance from view / Where I found peace from all hostility!"[469] That envy was more like resentment besides, for Petrarch next felt it towards heaven for snatching up Laura's soul, towards her soul's companions there for enjoying her holy company, and towards death for not taking him with her. Revisiting the countryside where Laura had left "her beautiful remains" behind on rising to heaven,[470] he fancied her in the lovers' sphere on high—more comely, less haughty, with only him and the body he had doted on still lacking. As against an eroticization of death, this was the eternalization of a chaste earthly reverence. More than for Petrarch, for Alessandro Adimari three centuries later women's beauty was by rights to be delighted in. Adimari devoted a cycle of fifty playful sonnets to female beauties each with a defect he forgave. His last two lovelies were dead and buried respectively: "To be as fair as you are at the last / Would Death itself die if it only could," he told the dead one,[471] and he assured the buried one that his ardor for her was only mounting in his memory now that she was reduced to ashes. Mario Praz cited this last sonnet as a seeming specimen of "romantic necrophilia" except that, being baroque, it was meant merely for shock effect.[472] Even so qualified, the equivalence is false, for on Adimari's facetious terms burial was a defect to be forgiven.[473]

The change from the old regime to the new can be seen in sharp relief as between two fictional heroines' deaths in the wilds of America seventy years apart. Manon Lescaut died swiftly, whereupon her doting lover kissed her goodbye and buried her within a single paragraph.[474] By way of contrast, Atala's moonlit funeral alone came to fully a tenth of her total story even after her painfully slow death. "Do not require me to describe my feelings to you," Manon's lover enjoined Prévost's readers. Atala's lover indulged Chateaubriand's readers the other way around. Yet *Atala* still spoke briefly to the Christian sensibility. "I was tempted to reopen the grave and see my beloved once again," Atala's lover related: "a religious fear restrained me." No religious fear was to restrain Chateaubriand's René at Amélie's Carmelite coffin just one year later.

When modern romances with death drew on premodern originals, the differences were telling. In Greek legend Achilles, having slain fierce Penthesilea in battle, fell upon her fair body impulsively despite its deadness at his first close sight of it. In Kleist's *Penthesilea* the live Amazon kissed Achilles to death with no more excuse to offer than that "kisses" rhymed with "bites" (*Küsse* with *Bisse*) as spoken in Kleist's Prusso-German. Again, when Keats poetized an ancient tale of a bride unmasked as a lamia, he gave it the single, eloquent twist that, even as she vanished, the groom's marriage robe became his winding sheet.[475] Keats changed nothing material in poetizing Boccaccio's Isabetta preserving her lover's severed head in a pot of basil; he did, though, make sweet moan for her all through his sorrowing verses where Boccaccio had spun out his yarn rather for chuckles and shudders.[476] Faust, a romantics' favorite, had a predecessor in Marlowe's Doctor Faustus, whose Mephostophilis conjured up dead Helen for him out of thin air—an apparition that vanished when he tried to kiss it.[477] Heine's Doctor Faust by contrast got more than he bargained for from his honest-to-goodness corpse of a Helen:

> You conjured me up from the grave
>   Through your magical will
> And filled me with hot glowing lust
>   You can no longer still.
> Oh, press your lips upon my lips.
>   Divine is human breath!
> I drink your soul out to the dregs.
>   The dead can't get enough.[478]

Here was carrion to be reckoned with.

But premodern exceptions there were—rare and isolated exceptions that thereby proved the rule. A cute literary case in point dates from around 1150, when a Flemish magistrate gave this inside story of a familiar gospel text: the tetrarch Herod loved his stepdaughter Salome, but Salome loved the preacher John, so jealous Herod presented Salome with John's severed head, which she longed to kiss except that it kept cursing her.[479] Like a steam engine invented in the Hellenistic age, this takeoff on the holy writ could not take off in its time as did Heine's seven centuries later. A near equivalent in art is a Death and the Maiden print of 1517 by Niklaus Manuel Deutsch in which the maiden, instead of recoiling in horror from the bone man, guides his hand up her skirts.[480] Or to probe a little, the ancient Athenians were a life-loving lot by and large, with no manifest taste for the macabre, yet in Sophocles' *Antigone* the heroine got herself entombed alive, her fiancé joining her, when she insisted on tending the exposed corpse of a brother slain as a rebel. Interpret this drama like a dream, conflating the cherished corpse, the "bridal vault,"[481] and the solidarity with the repressed, and the infratext reads like a decadent manifesto vindicating necrophilia.[482] To push the point just a little harder, *Antigone* has been more popular down the millennia than the same author's *King Oedipus*.

Back on the level of explicitness, one whole premodern cultural area and moment came within range of the nineteenth century's sepulchral sex: England in the early seventeenth century.[483] John Donne thought to get back at a recalcitrant mistress by burying a wreath of her hair around his arm and then haunting her lovemaking with his successful rival.[484] Closer to macabre modernity, John Suckling asked himself in ogling a woman what kind of death's head she would make.[485] Closer still was the finale of John Ford's *The Broken Heart* of 1633, with its coronation of a Queen of Sparta clothed as a bride beside her murdered bridegroom— even if she did die of a broken heart in the process, leaving the marriage unconsummated. "Death shall not separate us," she told her consort, and she deposited "one kiss on these cold lips, my last." The others on stage with her spoke the moral of the tale in unison, as if in advance translation from Zacharias Werner: "Love only reigns in death." But closest of all was indisputably *The Second Maiden's Tragedy* of 1611, probably by Tourneur.[486] In it a maiden fled an importunate tyrant into death. He, undaunted, had his men hack open her sepulcher, crying: "Death nor the marble prison my love sleeps in / Shall keep her body lockt up from mine arms." Citing the precedent of Herod the Great (Salome's forefather),[487] he caused her corpse to be conveyed to his palace, where, decked out in black velvet with jewels and a crucifix, it received full royal honors. Despite a song sounded within about moldering flesh in the night of death, he affirmed: "How pleasing art thou to us even in death. / I love thee yet above all women living / And shall do seven years hence"— Herod's limit. Finding her cheeks too pale nonetheless, he ordered them reddened. The rightful heir to his throne, disguised as a cosmetologist, applied a poisonous rouge to them such that the tyrant, upon kissing them, went down in howling agony, taunted by his triumphant rival: "O thou sacrilegious villain, / . . . / Do all things end with death and not thy lust? / Hast thou devised a new way to damnation, / More dreadful than the soul of any sin / Did ever pass yet between earth and hell?" Archaisms apart, this was a drama fit for the last fin de siècle except that the necrophilia (like the incest in John Ford's *'Tis Pity She's a Whore*) was after all presented as shocking perversion and sacrilege, with the deviant miscreant duly punished—which would have struck any public in the Yellow Nineties, Catholic converts foremost, as quaintly prudish.

Four

Its Sequel and Meaning

*P*hysical love beyond death: as has been noted in passing, this theme of nineteenth-century culture took many of its cues from folklore, where naïve beliefs about animate corpses survived and developed throughout the Christian era. In the course of a quarter-century or so after 1914 the love-death complex sank from high culture to low, thus approximately reverting to type.

Some of its enthusiasts from its pre–World War I heyday—Rachilde, Hanns Heinz Ewers, Lovis Corinth, Franz von Stuck, Alfred Kubin— went on mining it into the 1920s. Thomas Mann worked his way out of it beginning during the protracted carnage of 1914–18 by breaking the spell that love and death together cast over a young visitor to a sanatorium in *The Magic Mountain*. D. H. Lawrence turned it topsy-turvy by depicting sex as deadly depletion in *The Rainbow* of 1915 and *Women in Love* of 1920. The femme fatale was good and dated in the highbrow novel by the time of Pierre Benoît's vintage Saharan specimen of 1919.[488] Jean Cocteau surrealized the Orpheus legend on stage with death trebly foiled by love—with Orpheus getting both his head and his Eurydice back, plus immortality to boot.[489] Jean Anouilh countered with death preventing the love of Orpheus and Eurydice from growing stale,[490] but then for the Orpheus and Eurydice of Tennessee Williams death was even more brutal and implacable than for their Attic prototypes.[491] Jean Giraudoux dramatized the Judith story anew, with his heroine murdering her man to keep him from sleeping off his love for her[492]—hardly a sexual investment in death. William Faulkner's *A Rose for Emily*, with its skeleton in an old maid's bridal chamber, was a case of necrophilia but no case for it.[493] Georges Bataille kept his youthful necrophiliac fiction under wraps for a quarter century until he had established his respectability as a literary historian.[494] As late as the 1960s a couple's double death could still climax a great novel—not as a Wagnerian joy ride, though, but as the end term of a deep love that was found to be unlivable because the flesh is inherently inadequate and the spirit tormented by possessiveness.[495] Artists continued to sexualize Christ's death outright for some years after 1914; to take just Belgian examples, the three Marys desperately caressed an emaciated corpse in Albert Servaes, a sinewy Jesus with slicked-up hair glared boldly from the cross in Gustaaf van de Woestijne, and in George Minne the Madonna hugged her dead son flat on the ground of an empty, ghostly landscape.[496] Then Jesus resumed his classic decorum at the hands of a Max Slevogt, a Marc Chagall, a Salvador Dali, a Bernard Buffet.[497] Sex murder laid no claim to macabre charm in the art of George Grosz, of Heinrich Davringhausen, of Max Beckmann, of Otto Dix.[498] Dix juxtaposed sex and death in competitive ugliness in his *Still Life in the Studio* of 1924, with its obscene model gesticulating like a faceless dummy beside her. A rare Ophelia in art now came without tenderness, a rare Judith without femininity, rare Salomes without lewdness.[499] Francesca went by the boards.[500] The bone man reclaimed his old sexist monopoly as a death symbol in high art[501] even as German maidens blithely yielded to him in more popular depictions[502]—and flirted wickedly with him on bookmarks.[503] Folksy Margit Kovács sculpted two hapless lovers of Magyar legend buried together.[504] Die-hard local expressionists shown in Vienna as late as 1987 had raided the old repertory for a bosomy female nude writhing between agony and ecstasy, another topped with a death's head, and a stigmatic male corpse with an oversized penis; some had even gone new lengths to produce a wild erotic dance by Cain with Abel's skeleton, pendants of a couple in violent, animated intercourse and rigid, deathlike intercourse, and nine gory panels of Marat and Charlotte Corday mutilating each other in the bathroom.[505] Albert Belasco of London has glitzed up the old run of mythic-magical-macabre backdrops to a gaudy, over-exposed femme fatale on canvas. The Medusa, a fugitive from art, put in

Figure 57. The payoff for penitence. Albrecht Dürer, *The Elevation of Saint Magdalen*, 1504–5. (The Metropolitan Museum of Art, New York.)

Figure 58. Rejoining her bridegroom. Marco d'Oggiono, *The Magdalen Transported to Heaven*, 1520. (Galleria degli Uffizi, Florence.)

Figure 59. Consecrated to death. Francesco Furini, *The Penitent Magdalen*, c. 1630. (Staatsgalerie Stuttgart.)

Figure 60. A pious pinup. Marius Vasselon, *The Penitent Magdalen*, 1887. (Musée des Beaux-Arts, Tours.)

Figure 61. Demonstratively dead. Annibale Carracci, *Dead Christ*, 1606. (Staatsgalerie Stuttgart.)

Figure 62. Unmistakably dead. Hans Holbein, *Dead Christ*, 1531. (Öffentliche Kunstsammlung Basel, Kunstmuseum.)

Figure 63. LEFT: Weirdly dead. Giovanni Battista Rosso [Rosso Fiorentino], *The Dead Christ with Angels*, c. 1526. (Museum of Fine Arts, Boston.)
Figure 64. RIGHT: Unearthly love. Jacques Bellange, *Pietà*, 1615, after Michelangelo. (Graphische Sammlung Albertina, Vienna.)

Figure 65. LEFT: Nuptials deferred. Auguste Rodin, *Christ and the Magdalen,* c.
1894. (The Fine Arts Museum of San Francisco.)
Figure 66. RIGHT: Martyrdom in the modern mode. Emilio Franceschi, *Eulalia
Christiana,* 1887. (Civica Galleria d'Arte Moderna, Turin.)

Figure 67. LEFT: The impenitent Magdalen. Félicien Rops, *Christ's Lover,* 1887.
(Bibliothèque Royale Albert Ier, Cabinet des Estampes, Brussels.)
Figure 68. RIGHT: A sexy Savior. Gustaaf van de Woestijne, *Jesus Christ Offering
Us His Blood,* 1925. (Musées Royaux des Beaux-Arts, Brussels.)

Figure 69. A pop martyr. *Green Arrow,* 1989.

Figure 70. TOP: A pop Magdalen. Michael Zulli, *Taboo* No. 2, 1989. *Figure 71.* BOTTOM: Explicit. *Green Arrow* [*Necrophilia Manny*], 1989.

Figure 72. TOP: Deadly sexy. Mel Ramos, *Señorita Rio—The Queen of Spies*, 1963. (Louis K. Meisel Gallery, New York.)

Figure 73. BOTTOM: Death and the nonmaiden. *The Punisher*, Volume 1, Number 1, 1991, cover.

Figure 74. A pop vampire. *Vampirella: Morning in America,* Book 1, 1991, cover.

Figure 75. Vamping in a new medium. *Nosferatu*, Germany 1922. (Bettmann Archive, New York.)

Figure 76. Never say die. *Black Orpheus*, France, Italy, Brazil 1958. (Bettmann Archive, New York.)

Figure 77. The explosive love-and-death mix. *Classic Punisher*, Volume 1, Number 1, 1991.

a lusty-lethal appearance in science fiction.[506] Low-brow novels, grade-B movies, and (since the late 1930s) comic books have featured vampires and vamps, nameless girls crucified,[507] necrophiles,[508] killers packing guns and babes together, and just gun-packing babes for short. Tear a mask from gangland's top gun in a filmed comic strip and out comes sexpot Madonna dying.[509]

This banalization and crudification of eroticized death within popular culture has been progressive on balance. The best vampire films toppled from F. W. Murnau's artistic *Nosferatu* of 1922 through the artful 1931 *Dracula* starring Bela Lugosi to the artless *Son of Dracula* in 1943 and its numberless sequels.[510] The top love-in-cold-blood stories plummeted from Dashiell Hammett to James M. Cain or Mickey Spillane and on down. Loving to death has struck its lowest notes in the latest heavy-metal rock of Guns n' Roses, Metal Church, Metallica, Death Angel, the Necros, or Slayer,[511] at a classic remove from Billy Holiday's grand *Gloomy Sunday* of 1941 ("in death I'm caressing you"). Necrophilia proper can still get some literary styling from an Yves Navarre or a Toni Morrison.[512] But the brothel variety dramatized by Jean Genet fast devolved onto the comic screen of Luis Buñuel,[513] and now the statue variety has gone back to church with Madonna embracing Jesus off a crucifix in her 1989 video number "Just like a Prayer." Cinematically, the lovers' double death, epic in *The Eternal Return* of 1943, still poignant in *Elvira Madigan* of 1967, somersaulted into the superorgasm of Pedro Aldomóvar's spoof of the sex-death nexus, *Matador* of 1986. Death as climactic bliss has sunk to the slang of "It's to die from!" Acting out has been on the rise, with a notable cult figure in Pasolini, who courted death as a supreme sexual experience. Pretended inside stories of sex murderers are hard to tell from the fiction sold beside them on drugstore racks. Or perhaps the real rise has been in interacting—in fantasy spilling over into reality spilling over into fantasy. John Hinkley went gunning for Ronald Reagan in hopes of impressing a starlet from a movie about a New York cab driver who went gunning for pimps while raving against smutty sex in the same vein as New York's serial killer of fetching girls and dating couples, David Berkowitz, alias Son of Sam.[514] And cultic satanism linked Berkowitz to Charlie Manson, whose clan slaughtered a pregnant starlet and her Hollywood party only to bloody her front door with a snatch of the Beatles' White Album containing *Happiness Is a Warm Gun*: "When

. . . I feel my finger on your trigger / I know no one can do me any harm."[515] The interplay is less roundabout in "snuff films" (live footage of sex murders) worked into home videos. But even on the lowest pop level such brushes with reality remain fringe effects.[516]

Death livening sex, sex livening death: it all goes back to Sardanapalus and Sade, but no farther. Premodern folk tales of sex beyond death were never voluptuous, only chilling. Modern elite culture turned that chilling into thrilling for an eager public, then backed away. Popular culture followed closely along until it took off on its own in our century. But wherever the shaky line between high and low culture is drawn, the love-death hybrid was bred above it.

Does this matter psychohistorically? Western culture has been now more, now less stratified at different times and places. The key consideration here is that the cultural elites who blended love and death in fantasy did so for a responsive public. It may be questioned how seriously they ever meant that blend or how seriously their public ever took it. The decadents at all odds preened themselves on their artificiality, and probably no comic-book reader or moviegoer suspends disbelief altogether. No matter: a nagging waking fantasy is as meaningful as any dream we shrug off while dreaming.

That nagging fantasy of love beyond death pushed hard against the dominant Western belief that with death the body loses all sensation, at least until Judgment Day. It projected earthly erotism beyond death—often grotesquely and fretfully, sometimes with tongue in cheek, mostly just symbolically or for the first postmortem hours or months, yet insistently, and in ever-new forms or variations. Equivalent conceptions, with practices to match, informed the ancient Oriental mystery cults.[517] They survive in popular Hinduism's libidinal cult of Kali, goddess of death. They are widespread among primitives, outright necrophilia inclusive.[518] Indeed, sex is joined to death ritually and symbolically the world over. Promiscuous sexual orgies are the rule at funerals among the Duyaks of Borneo, the Bara of Madagascar, the Dinka of the southern Sudan.[519] All see dying as rejoining the ancestral collectivity or being born outwards from this world. The Bara accordingly bury corpses the way babies are born—head first.[520] The Hindus, the Daribi, the Etero, and the Bara among other peoples regulate sex in keeping with their view of it as a deadly bodily drain, indeed as the primal source of death—with the woman to blame besides, as in the myth of Eve alias the femme fatale. The nineteenth-century Western love-death mix can be matched anthropologically in this way, element for element, many times over. The bulk of it can also be identified in the Western archaic heritage itself, of which many fragments led an underground existence throughout the Christian era before resurfacing among the romantics. But a crucial difference from alien or archaic equivalents stands out. As a rule, the modern Western intermix of love and death was not performative; it was fantasy only. The disparity between belief and behavior is an understated peculiarity of European culture. The Greeks already preached moderation and practiced excess. No sooner was Europe Christianized than it left the true practice of Christianity to so-called fanatics on the edges of normalcy. Here too, in its impracticality, the nineteenth century's sex-and-death fantasy was continuous with Christianity. And it is with this continuity beneath the radical rift from the one fantasy to the other that an analysis of love beyond death must begin.

"Must" here has a polemical edge to it. Should not the analysis of a mass fantasy conjoining love and death take off from Freudian considerations of eros as a derivative of the death instinct with an inherent tendency to revert to type? No, it should not. Such fundamentalizing, valid or not, is irrelevant to historic change. (Conversely, the climactic conjunction of eros and death in the culture surrounding them was highly relevant to Ferenczi's and Freud's speculations, begun in 1913, about a primal death instinct informing eros.)[521] Then should not the analysis of a mass fantasy at least explore its instinctual basis in the individuals who entertained it? The origin of this mass fantasy in individual sadomasochism is axiomatic for most observers.[522] And yet that cruel hangup shows nowhere in the lives or works of so many of the writers, artists, or composers involved—of Novalis, of Keats, of Heine, of Leopardi, of Rilke, to name just a few poets. From Chateaubriand to Poe, from Schubert to Berlioz, from Turgenev to Swinburne, from Delacroix to Munch, from Wilde to D'Annunzio, emotional constitutions differed as did backgrounds, upbringings, formative experiences. And in any case the decisive consideration is not the writers, artists, or composers who fashioned that fantasy, but the vast, psychologically heterogeneous public that snatched it up. To suppose that the death drive in the human breed in the West suddenly rose beginning around 1775 would be gratuitous. Nor will it do to argue that the death drive encroached on erotic fantasizing for want of large-scale bloodletting to drain it over the century before 1914, for the myth of love beyond death shaped up in all its essentials over the two decades and more of mass warfare set off by the French Revolution. To look for changes in parenting or domestic arrangements tending to induce latent sadomasochism in childhood would be an exercise in futility, sexual fixations being accidental for all practical purposes. And again, neither sadomasochism nor any other distinctive personal proclivity went into the making, or taking, of the love-death mix anyhow. The historic turnabout from death versus love to loving death in the Western mindset was, in a word, impersonal—a shared fantasm, meaning a collective phenomenon intelligible only as such.

As a shared fantasm it was of a kind with Christianity. More, it developed in Christendom when Christianity lost its hold as gospel about this world and the next, and for over a century it replaced the sexless Christian salvation with a lusty erotic thrust into death. That is, Christian spiritual love beyond death reappeared as post-Christian fleshly love beyond death: Jean Delville's *Love of Souls*, with its lovers' bodily embrace, is emblematic. Taken in isolation, the ephemeral reappearance of a defunct mass fantasy in new guise may invite any number of hypothetical explanations. But the core elements of the Christian creed have all been reappearing that way over the past two centuries. Thus the Christian eternity metamorphosed into the nineteenth-century notion that the past inhabits the present here and now; the Christian truth behind worldly appearances about-faced around 1900 into the truth of appearances themselves without a reality behind them; original sin came back in the ubiquitous twentieth-century vision of life as a delayed death sentence.[523] Through our post-Christian culture we have been reliving the Christian experience unconsciously in fragments. Love beyond death is one such fragment.

This unconscious reliving is the first and last word of the psychohistorical story of love beyond death. The words in between cannot be read clearly from the evidence to hand alone. The new afterlife fantasy derived from its Christian original in full, mostly by simple reversal, yet it also drew on non-Christian folklore, probably on pre-Christian myths and rituals. Thus vampirism was of a kind with the holy mass or communion, itself like the enthused devouring of a sacrificial god-figure to attain life immortal. But too little is known of Europe's religious prehistory to fit such pieces firmly together. The new, substitutive afterlife fantasy carried little logical conviction, but not because of the look of preposterousness it wears for the critical observer today. Poets as bright as we are, from Keats to Rilke, could sensualize death despite the contradiction in terms. Doctrinal absurdities exceeding that one engaged the church fathers, the medieval scholastics, the Protestant reformers. The ardent silliness of the fin-de-siècle cult of Salome in particular smacks of religious caricature. But loving death was never formulated doctrinally as was Christianity. It was a cluster of shared devotions and symbols bearing on human ulti-mates—like a primitive religion indeed, but one held loosely, with little solemnity, and frequently alongside the Christianity it contradicted. It is now failing after Christianity failed, but in the dissimilar way of sinking into mass culture with its brutal, frightful components escalated. It has come full circle back to the Marquis de Sade and Monk Lewis with heightened intensity—full spiral.

The chronology is suggestive. Lewis wrote and Sade rewrote during the French Reign of Terror, which spawned a pornography of death. Gentler inspirations blended with theirs into the complex of loving death. But even initially the destructive inspirations predominated, and the later the more, from Büchner and Poe to D'Annunzio and Mirbeau. Only weeks into World War I, wildly welcomed by a Europe that glamorized death, the deglamorization began. By 1945 at the latest, with Hitler's death camps exposed and two A-bombs exploded, the deglamorization should have been complete. And complete it was by then for the elites: they no longer swooned for loving death but felt instead, with Philip Larkin, "the dread / Of dying, of being dead," of there being "no sight, no sound, / No touch or taste or smell, nothing to think with, / Nothing to love or link with."[524]

At the same time, bits and pieces of loving death survived with the vast juvenile public of all ages, evolving into ever-starker visions of sex and slaughter conjoined. However—and much hinges on this huge "however"—the escalation of the destructiveness in such mixed visions since 1914 has been part and parcel of an escalation of destructive visions generally. Visions of human destruction have in fact been predominantly sex-free from Goya and Géricault on. Death minus the Maiden haunted the music of Dmitri Shostakovitch in our times. And death has meanwhile been crowding out even the nonmaidens of popular culture. The sex in killer stories has been perfunctory or extraneous if even that.[525] "The Killers" by Ernest Hemingway or Dashiell Hammett's *Red Harvest* are models of their loveless kind. The 1976 movie *Bonnie and Clyde*, a killers' romance, culminated in the killers' massacre. Westerns and war stories, from gang wars to star wars, do still better with just guys and no dolls. Animated cartoons have purveyed sex-free mayhem since the Disney days. Gore has been the life blood of the newer horror movies.[526] A heavy-metal chorus runs: "Ripping apart, severing flesh, gouging eyes, tearing limb from limb."[527] Guns have been sexualized outright in the photography of Larry Clark and others.[528] Christ's passion itself has come into the comics with the merest passing glimpse of a lewd Magdalen.[529] In sum, the slaughter component of the love-death mix has been swelled since 1914 by an independent upswing of visions of death and destruction. This separate development lies outside the scope of an inquiry into the fantasm of love beyond death, except for the need to factor it out. This done, that hybrid fantasm appears to have fairly run its course. Like another post-Christian fantasm, that of a continuing presence of the past,[530] it was a failed compensation for the lost Christian afterworld. As such, it has gone the way of Christianity itself.

Notes

1. Mario Praz *La carne, la morte e il diavolo nella letteratura romantica* 1930, 1942, 1976; tr. *The Romantic Agony* 1933, 1951, 1970.

2. Ariès *L'homme* 79–90, *Images* 217. Ariès's evidence in this line is uncharacteristically skimpy and dubious.

3. Vovelle 585.

4. Zacharias Werner *Psyche: Galatea* 1809: "liebender Tod." Werner preached the unity of life and death in love, for God "joins what flowed from him: the double life" ("eint, was ihm entquoll, das Doppelleben"): "Der steinerne Bräutigam und sein Liebchen" 1807.

5. "Amor e morte" 1832–33. Further, *Lettere* (1949) 1053: "And certainly love and death are the only beautiful things the world has, and the very only ones worth desiring" (16 August 1832).

6. MacKay 123 and passim.

7. Dante Gabriel Rossetti "Death-in-Love" *The House of Life* 1869.

8. "Les deux bonnes soeurs" 1842: "d'affreuses douceurs." Echoed by old Hugo: Praz 25.

9. *La tentation de Saint Antoine* 1874.

10. 1889: quoted by Henri Mitterand "Étude" in Émile Zola *Les Rougon-Macquart* IV (Paris: Gallimard 1966) 1737 from Zola's notes for *La bête humaine* cf. Zola *La bête humaine* 1889–90: "They took each other, finding love at the pit of death with the voluptuous anguish of beasts tearing each other apart when in heat"; etc.

11. "Extase" *Au jardin de l'infante* 1893.

12. "Le suaire" *Histoires magiques* 1894.

13. "Conte des faucheurs" 1895: Birkett 222.

14. *Le jardin des supplices* 1899.

15. *Amori et dolori sacrum* 1903.

16. *Hymnen an die Nacht* 1800.

17. "Der Jüngling und der Tod" 1817 lyrics by Franz von Spaun.

18. "Der Müller und der Bach" and "Des Baches Wiegenlied" *Die schöne Müllerin* 1823 after Wilhelm Müller 1816–20. "Der Lindenbaum" *Die Winterreise* 1827 after Wilhelm Müller 1823: "Hier findest du deine Ruh!"

19. "Ode to a Nightingale" 1819.

20. "To Autumn" 1819.

21. "Der Tod, das ist die kühle Nacht" *Buch der Lieder* 1824, Brahms 1884.

22. "Ahnung" by 1830: "In des Todes kalten Armen / Kann das Leben erst erwarmen."

23. "Amor e morte" 1832–33: "la gentilezza del morir."

24. *Raphaël* 1849.

25. "Out of the Cradle Endlessly Rocking" 1859/81.

26. *Le livre du néant* 1868/72 ("Quel étrange besoin de se sentir morts"); "Mensonges" *L'illusion* 1875 ("Ton oeil est bleu, clair et limpide, / Comme l'eau d'un étang profond; / L'eau des étangs bleus est perfide, / La mort attirante est au fond"); *Le livre du néant* 1868/72 ("Tu es belle comme la Mort dans un jour de batailles").

27. "Musique confidentielle," "Silence! . . . ," "Tentation" 1893: "Le désir / De mourir / Comme une extase en nous monte"; "Il est des soirs d'agonie / Où l'on rêve la mort bénie / Au long d'une étreinte infinie"; "Le silence et l'oubli dans l'éternel repos."

28. "La chimère" by 1895 (on Moreau's painting so named): quoted Jean Lorrain "Un étrange jongleur" *Sensations et souvenirs* 1895.

29. *Le livre des masques* 1896: Birkett 179.

30. *Les hors nature* 1897: Birkett 179.

31. *Von der Armuth und vom Tode* 1905: "Der große Tod, den jeder in sich hat, / Das ist die Frucht, um die sich alles dreht."

32. "To the Sunset Goddess" *Poèmes I* 1910.

33. 1909, 1910; cf. "Der Abschied" *Das Lied von der Erde* 1907–9.

34. "Der Schläfer im Walde," "Der Tod der Liebenden" *Der ewige Tag* 1911.

35. "Sunday Morning" 1915.

36. "Elegie" 1872–80. Those white-clad maidens also danced for Puvis de Chavanne in his *Death and the Maidens* 1872.

37. *Die Nachtwachen des Bonaventura* 1804.

38. 1818.

39. "The Murders in the Rue Morgue" 1841.

40. 1868–69.

41. An especially gruesome derivative was Jan Van Beeks *Long Live Death* 1873.

42. *Buried Alive* 1854; cf. Consuelo Fould's sexier *Buried Alive* 1898.

43. "Rettungslos" 1903.

44. *Madame Potiphar* 1831.

45. Henry Peach Robinson *Fading Away* 1858.

46. Dijkstra 50–56. Similarly, Böcklin *Dead Girl's Head* 1879.

47. See especially *The Scream* pastel 1893, *Woman on the Seashore* colored woodcut 1898, *Head of a Girl on the Shore* colored woodcut 1899, and *The Dance of Life* 1899–1900.

48. *Weltende* 1911.

49. The second of his *Michelangelo Gedichte* 1897.

50. *Morgue und andere Gedichte* 1912.

51. *Der ewige Tag* 1911.

52. *Essai sur la littérature anglaise* 1836: quoted Honour 275.

53. "Ophélie" 1870: "Sur l'onde calme et noire où dorment les étoiles."

54. "Pauvres petites Ophélie" 1897: "sous l'eau glauque aux tièdes remous."

55. *Les vierges* 1896: "Tumulte inextricable où sa tête s'est prise; / Est-ce le lin d'un champ, est-ce sa chevelure? / L'embrouillamini vert qui rouit autour d'elle . . ."

56. "Ophelia" *Der ewige Tag* 1911.

57. Paintings 1838, 1844, 1853, lithograph 1843, drawings 1853.

58. 1851–52; cf. James John Baptiste Bertrand *Ophelia's Death* 1872.

59. By 1900.

60. Numerous versions 1901–9.

61. 1842–70.

62. C. 1881.

63. "La jeune Tarantine" by 1794.

64. 1871.

65. 1847.

66. 1849–50; cf. Turner's 1808 print *The Fifth Plague of Egypt* and Louis Ridel *Shipwrecked (L'épave)* 1907.

67. Rainer Maria Rilke *Die Aufzeichnungen des Malte Laurids Brigge* 1911.

68. See Dijkstra 42–46 for nifty examples—but Homer Watson's *The Death of Elaine* 1877 tops them all.

69. Dijkstra 56–60, 62–63.

70. *La morte amoureuse* 1836.

71. *Les déracinés* 1897: Praz 287.

72. Georges Callot *The Death of the Little Courtesan* 1901.

73. *Le crépuscule des nymphes* 1898.

74. Dijkstra 46.

75. *Le trajet* c. 1911.

76. 1863.

77. "Ashes of Soldiers" 1865/81; further, "A sight in camp in the daybreak gray and dim" and "Reconciliation."

78. 1855–56.

79. 1891.

80. "Morgue" *Neue Gedichte* 1910: "Die Augen haben hinter ihren Lidern / Sich umgewandt und schauen jetzt hinein."

81. Jules Amédée Barbey d'Aurevilly *Léa* 1832: quoted Praz 33.

82. "A Feast during the Plague" 1830 in Pushkin *Little Tragedies* finely translated by Eugene M. Kayden.

83. "Introduction" 1831.

84. "The Philosophy of Composition" 1846.

85. 1838, 1848, 1849.

86. Fiedler 267, 269; cf. MacKay 125–27 on Dickens's "Nellicide" in England.

87. 1879, 1902.

88. Quoted Maigron 181.

89. "L'amante macabre" and "Mademoiselle Squelette" *Les névroses* 1883.

90. 1870; 1891; c. 1899.

91. "Un amateur d'âmes" *Du sang, de la volupté et de la mort* 1893: Praz 286.

92. "A la fille aimée" *Poèmes I* 1910.

93. *Die Nachtwachen des Bonaventura* 1804.

94. *La peau de chagrin* 1831: Dijkstra 38–39.

95. *The Sleep of Endymion* 1793.

96. *Aurora and Cephalus* 1810.

97. *Amor and Psyche* 1817.

98. *Odalisque* c. 1845–50; cf. Pierre Bonnard *Woman Dozing on a Bed* 1899.

99. *Ariadne* 1868.

100. 1868, 1872, c. 1894, c. 1895. On Leighton's drowsing ladies: Bendiner 121–43.

101. 1876. On sleep = death: Georg Heym "Schwarze Visionen" *Der ewige Tag* 1911 and Dijkstra 60–63, 64–82. For the archaic and classical roots of this equation: Vermeule 145–72 passim.

102. c. 1875, 1875, 1882, 1887.

103. 1886 sculpture.

104. 1873–90.

105. 1904 (photograph).

106. Matthew Gregory Lewis *The Monk* 1796.

107. *René* 1802.

108. *The Death of Sardanapalus* 1827; cf. Max Slevogt *Sardanapalus* 1907, centered in a comely corpse positioned as if for sex.

109. "The Fall of the House of Usher" 1839.

110. "Une charogne" 1842–46.

111. "Le séduisant croquemort": Praz 124.

112. "The Leper" 1857.

113. 1862.

114. 1889 preface to Rachilde *Monsieur Vénus* 1884: Praz 258.

115. "Les tombales" 1891.

116. *Le livre de Monelle* 1894.

117. *Amori et dolori sacrum* 1903: Praz 288.

118. "Fleur de cinq-pierres" *Coeur double* 1891: Praz 282.

119. "Amour d'hopital" *La nuit* 1897: Praz 210–11.

120. *Le jardin des supplices* 1899: Birkett 251.

121. *Monsieur de Phocas: Astarté* 1901: Birkett 201–7.

122. 1797.

123. Zacharias Werner "Der Ritter von Sidon" *Die Kreuzesbrüder* 1807: "Denn Lieb' ist der ewigen Stärke Gesell, / Die reißet das Leben heiter und schnell / Zum Grabe."

124. Catulle Mendès *Zo'har* 1886: Praz 256–57.

125. "Die Welt ist so schön," "Mein süßes Lieb," "Kennst du das alte Liedchen . . ." *Lyrisches Intermezzo* 1827.

126. "Romantyczność" c. 1822; "Eine Erscheinung" c. 1850. The heroine of Kerner's *Die Seherin von Prevorst* 1829 goes into a lifelong intermittent trance after dreaming that a dead preacher is in bed with her.

127. 1831.

128. 1841.

129. "Les cydalises" *Odelettes* 1848: "Où sont nos amoureuses? / Elles sont au tombeau."

130. *La tentation de Saint Antoine* 1849.

131. Ibid.

132. *Le roman de la momie* 1857.

133. "John Hamilton Llewellens Ende" 1905.

134. Victor Scheffel "Hugideo" 1857.

135. "Willowwood I" 1868.

136. Fernand Desnoyers "L'amant des morts" *Vers fantastiques* 1869.

137. *The Anatomist* 1869. Jean Jacques Henner matched this cadaver but put a patriarchal gaze upon it in *The Levite of Ephraim and His Dead Wife* 1898.

138. *Monsieur Vénus* 1884: Birkett 164.

139. Joséphin Péladan *Istar* 1888: Birkett 150–51.

140. "Morella" 1835.

141. "Ulalume" 1847.

142. "Ligeia" 1838.

143. "Berenice" 1835.

144. "La chevelure" 1884.

145. 1841.

146. *Die Marquise von O . . .* 1808.

147. "Der Sandmann" 1817.

148. *Une histoire sans nom* 1882.

149. *Florentinische Nächte* 1835.

150. *La Vénus d'Ille* 1837.

151. *Venus im Pelz* 1870.

152. *L'oeuvre* 1886.

153. "The Happy Prince" 1888.

154. "La femme de marbre" 1900: Dijkstra 148–49.

155. "Charmides" 1881.

156. "Véra" 1874–80 *Contes cruels* 1883.

157. Mary Shelley *Frankenstein* 1818 ("a shroud enveloped her form, and I saw the graveworms crawling on the folds of the flannel").

158. "Mir träumte von einem Königskind" 1827.

159. *Là-bas* 1891.

160. *La sanglante ironie* 1891: Birkett 164.

161. Henry Fuseli *Wolfram Watching His Wife in Her Cell* c. 1815 (illustrating Marguerite de Navarre's *Heptameron* of 1558).

162. "La marquise de Spolète" *Princesses d'ivoire et d'ivresse* 1902.

163. *Novembre* 1842: Praz 160.

164. "Le monstre" 1866.

165. "By the city dead-house" 1867.

166. *Die Nachtwachen des Bonaventura* 1804.

167. *Our Mutual Friend* 1864–65.

168. *Lenore: The Return from the Army* 1829, *Lenore: The Dead Ride Fast* 1830; *The Ballad of Lenore* 1839; *Lenore* 1891.

169. André Robert Andréa de Nercéat *Les aphrodites*.

170. *Die Nachtwachen des Bonaventura* 1804.

171. *Wanda, Königin der Samariten* 1809: "Leben ist der Liebe Spiel; / Tod der Liebe Weg zum Ziel."

172. *Reiseschatten* 1811 ("Nachspiel der zweiten Schattenreihe"): "So Leben endlich wir im Tod erlangen!"

173. *Romanzen von Rosenkranz* 1812.

174. "The Improvisatore" 1821.

175. *Death's Jest-Book* 1827.

176. "The Phantom-Wooer" by 1837.

177. "Love's Last Messages" by 1837.

178. "Chant d'amour" 1822.

179. "Élégie" 1825.

180. "Mein süßes Lieb" *Lyrisches Intermezzo* 1827.

181. *Symphonie fantastique* (finale) 1830.

182. [Évariste Boulay-Paty] *Élie Mariaker* 1834: IV: XVI.

183. *Dantons Tod* 1835.

184. *Leonce und Lena* by 1837.

185. *La danse des morts* 1838.

186. *Wuthering Heights* 1847.

187. *Sonnets from the Portuguese* 1850.

188. "Billet du matin" *Contemplations* 1856.

189. "Le Léthé" 1857.

190. "La mort des amants" 1856: "des divans profonds comme des tombeaux."

191. "Der Tod der Liebenden" *Der ewige Tag* 1911: "Wir werden immer bei einander bleiben."

192. "Septima" *Vies imaginaires* 1896.

193. "Danaëtte" *Histoires magiques* 1898.

194. "Jezebel" 1899.

195. *Et toujours! Et jamais!* 1859/63; see Stump 34 and passim. This statue paralleled a contemporary poem of unknown authorship about a lover welcoming his sweetheart into death: ibid. 34 and n. 18.

196. *Mammon* 1884–85; *Love Triumphant* 1899–1900.

197. *Love* 1894–96. Comparably, Jean Dampt in 1896 carved an oak bed inscribed "Sad as a tomb, or joyous as a love nest": Silverman 224.

198. *Satan's Treasures* 1895.

199. *Notre Dame de Paris* 1831.

200. Nercéat 1793.

201. *Hymnen an die Nacht* 1800.

202. Bonaventura 1804.

203. Johann Peter Hebel "Unverhofftes Wiedersehen" 1811—which inspired E. T. A. Hoffmann's tale "Die Bergwerke von Falun" 1818 and Hugo von Hofmannsthal's drama *Das Bergwerk zu Falun* 1899.

204. *The Giaour* 1813.

205. *Lyrisches Intermezzo* 1827.

206. "The Oblong Box" 1844.

207. *La dame aux camélias* 1848.

208. "La tombe" 1884.

209. *Mardi* 1849.

210. *Aurélia* 1855.

211. *Clara Militch* 1882.

212. *Le jardin de Bérénice* 1891; *Le culte du moi* 1888–91.

213. "A una morta" 1907.

214. *Sogno d'un mattino di primavera* 1907.

215. "Der Tod der Geliebten" *Neue Gedichte* 1910.

216. 1866–68, touched up 1886; 1897; "Isabella and the Pot of Basil" 1818, after Boccaccio *Decameron* 1348–53.

217. Bonaventura 1804.

218. *Florentinische Nächte* 1835.

219. "Berenice" 1835, "Eleonora" 1841, "Morella" 1835.

220. "Posthuma" 1849.

221. "Maud-Evelyn" 1900.

222. "Clara Militch" 1882.

223. *La nouvelle Héloïse* 1761.

224. *Palingenesien* 1798.

225. "Dein Angesicht so lieb und schön . . ." *Lyrisches Intermezzo* 1822–23, set to music by Robert Schumann 1840–51.

226. *Symphonie fantastique* 1830.

227. *The Monk* 1796.

228. *Attila, König der Hunnen* 1808.

229. 1808.

230. *Undine* 1811.

231. "Die traurige Hochzeit" 1813.

232. *Die Schuld* 1813.

233. *Ahnung und Gegenwart* 1811/15, *Le rouge et le noir* 1830.

234. Pushkin fragment 1825, then "Egipetskie nochi" 1835; *Mademoiselle de Maupin* 1835, then *Cléopâtre* 1845: Praz 152–54.

235. "Porphyria's Lover" 1836.

236. "Demon" 1839.

237. "Une martyre" 1842.

238. "Anactoria" 1863–65.

239. "Lucretius" 1868.

240. "Le rideau cramoisi" *Les diaboliques* 1874.

241. *Il trionfo della morte* 1890. (Praz 199: D'Annunzio relished inflicting slow, painful death on sexy heroines, preferably by burning them alive.)

242. *La bête humaine* 1890.

243. *L'histoire tragique de la princesse Phénissa* 1894.

244. *Aphrodite* 1896.

245. *Ballad of a Barber* 1896.

246. *The Ballad of Reading Gaol* 1898.

247. *Le jardin des supplices* 1899.

248. *Monsieur de Phocas: Astarté* 1901.

249. *Love* 1908: Dijkstra 400–401—plausibly retitled *Judith and Holofernes* in the catalogue raisonné Oskar A. Müller *Albert von Keller 1844 Gais/Schweiz-1920 München* 1981.

250. *Mörder, Hoffnung der Frauen* 1909.

251. *Tragedy* bas relief 1912.

252. "Auf den Wolken" 1830: "Küßt mir aus der Brust das Leben!"

253. "Le voyage à Cythère" 1851.

254. "A Ballad of Death" 1865.

255. *Chastebard* 1865.

256. *Lesbia Brandon* 1864–78. Bertie's tutor had it both ways: "Deeply he desired to die by her, if that could be; and more deeply, if this could be, to destroy her."

257. Praz 201–4.

258. *Le martyre de Saint Sébastien* 1911, set to music by Debussy.

259. *Le livre du néant* 1868/72 ("Si dans une coupe j'avais pu mettre la pureté de tes yeux, les douceurs de tes seins, et les boire, et mourir,—l'âme tout embaumée de toi!").

260. "La ventouse" *Les névroses* 1881: "c'est tout l'homme qui nourrit la ventouse."

261. "Le succube" ibid.: "Viens! tout mon coeur tari te convoite en mourant!"

262. *Le jardin des supplices* 1899.

263. 1905–8.

264. *Der fliegende Holländer* 1843, *Tristan und Isolde* 1857–59 (cf. Jean Delville *Tristan and Isolt* drawing 1887).

265. *Wanda, Königin der Samariten* 1809: "Ha!—Er lebt!—Ich kann ihn töten, / Liebend mit ihm untergehn." (Further: "So stürben wir, um ungetrennt, /

Ewig einig, ohne End', / Ohn' Erwachen, ohn' Erbangen, / Namenlos in Lieb'
umfangen, / Ganz uns selbst gegeben, / Der Liebe nur zu leben.")

266. "Les amants de Montmorency" 1830; "La mort des amants" 1857.

267. "Die Flucht" 1830; "Jammertal" by 1856.

268. *Lelio ou le retour à la vie* 1831—the sequel to *Symphonie fantastique*.

269. "If I were loved" 1833.

270. 1833.

271. "The Fall of the House of Usher" 1839.

272. "Les noyades" by 1865.

273. *Le livre du néant* 1868/72.

274. *La tentation de Saint Antoine* 1874.

275. *Akëdysséril* 1886.

276. *Axël* 1889 (posthumous).

277. *Rome* 1896.

278. *Parisina* 1913.

279. *Leap from the Cliff* 1833.

280. *Finis* etching 1881; cf. Munch *The Dead Loving Couple* drawing 1896–97.

281. 1871; 1900.

282. *Otello* 1887.

283. *El sentimiento trágico de la vida en los hombres y los pueblos* 1913.

284. *Le livre du néant* 1868/72.

285. "To Helen" 1849.

286. "Hymne à la beauté" 1860: "un moribond caressant son tombeau."

287. *Certains* 1889.

288. Adelbert von Chamisso *Frauen-Liebe und Leben* 1830 (Schumann 1840):
"O laß im Traume mich sterben / Gewieget an seiner Brust."

289. "Fatima" 1833. Heroines felt this way as late as Thomas Hardy *Tess of
the d'Urbervilles* 1891: "Her one desire" was "to make herself his" and "then, if
necessary, to die."

290. "Chanson des amoureuses" *Les névroses* 1883: "Nos soupirs s'en vont
dans la tombe."

291. *Pasqua di Gea* 1891: "bene è che si muoja / quando tu giungi al fine."

292. Paul Verlaine *Femmes* 1890: "frais comme des tombeaux" (after the act).

293. "Destins" *Au jardin de l'infante* 1893: "Tes bras, tes bras profonds et doux
comme la mort."

294. "Tentation" ibid.: "Dis, lorsque tu collais tes lèvres à sa bouche, / Dis,
n'as-tu pas vécu parfois, dans un moment, / L'infini d'une angoisse éperdue et
farouche? / . . . C'est alors que tu baisais ma bouche, ô mon amant." Likewise,
in Zacharie Astruc *Les 14 stations du Salon 1859 suivies d'un récit douloureux* 1859

Death had told the Maiden: "I took the kiss you meant for him" ("J'ai recueilli le baiser qui lui était destiné").

295. *The mors et vita Agony* c. 1870.

296. *Big Death Scene* 1905.

297. Gustave Moreau *The Suitors* 1852–98 (unfinished).

298. Herbert James Draper *The Lament for Icarus* 1898.

299. Johann August Apel and Friedrich August Laun "Die Totenbraut" 1810.

300. Pétrus Borel "Don Andrée Vésalius l'anatomiste" *Champavert: Contes immoraux* 1833.

301. Henry James "The Altar of the Dead" 1895. All his life James made notes for an equally unclassifiable story of a woman whose long-awaited husband "comes in the form of death": Fiedler 304.

302. Remy de Gourmont "Le cierge adultère" *Histoires magiques* 1894.

303. Heinrich August Ossendorfer "Der Vampir."

304. "Die Braut von Korinth" 1797.

305. Significant texts featuring vampirism and the like, beyond those to be cited next, include Novalis *Hymnen an die Nacht* 1800 ("O sauge, Geliebter . . ."), Robert Southey "Thalaba the Destroyer" 1800, Jan Potocki *Le manuscrit trouvé à Saragosse* 1803–15, Charles Robert Maturin *Melmoth the Wanderer* 1820, E. T. A. Hoffmann *Serapionsbrüder* 1821, Charles Nodier *Smarra* 1821 and *Trilby* 1822, Ernst Raupach *Laßt die Toten ruhn* 1823, Prosper Mérimée "Cara-Ali le vampire" *La Guzla* 1827 and *Lokis* 1869, Theodor Hildebrand *Der Vampir oder die Totenbraut* 1828, Henry Liddell "The Vampire Bride" 1833, Nikolai Gogol *Vij* 1835, Théophile Gautier *La morte amoureuse* 1836, James Clerk Maxwell "The Vampyre" 1845, Thomas Preskett Prest(?) *Varney the Vampire* 1847, Alexandre Dumas *Le vampire* 1851, Ivan Turgenev *Prizraki* (Apparitions) 1863, Lautréamont *Les chants de Maldoror* by 1870, Sheridan Le Fanu *Carmilla* 1872, Guy de Maupassant *Le horla* 1887, Eric Stanislaus, Count Stenbock "The True Story of a Vampire" *Studies of Death* 1894, Ossip Schubin *Vollmondzauber* 1899, Hanns Heinz Ewers *Alraune* 1911, F. Marion Crawford "For the Blood Is the Life" *Uncanny Tales* 1911, and E. F. Benson "The Room in the Tower" 1912. Vampires were painted by Philip Burne-Jones *The Vampire* 1897, sculpted by Franz Flaun *Vampire* c. 1904, and engraved abundantly by Félicien Rops, Gustave Doré, and Eduardo de Albertis. Three reference works characteristic of their times are Dom Augustin Calmet *Dissertation sur les apparitions des anges, des démons, et des esprits et sur les revenans et vampires de Hongrie, de Bohème, de Moravie, et de Silésie* 1746 (esp. 291, 404–6, 418–19), Jacques Collin de Plancy *Dictionnaire infernal* 1818, and Jules Bois *Le satanisme et la magie* 1895.

306. Polidori's novelette also spawned countless stageplays and at least one opera: Heinrich Marschauer *Der Vampyr* 1828.

307. *Studies in the History of the Renaissance* 1873.

308. Dijkstra 348.

309. The equivalence blood = semen in fantasies of being sucked dry was first noted by Jones 98–130.

310. Nercéat 1793. Further: Bentley 26–30; Gagnier 144–45; Griffin 142; Tracy 42, 54; Twitchell "Myth" 112–13.

311. Baudelaire "Les métamorphoses du vampire" 1852, "Le vampire" 1855, "Le poison" 1857; Munch *Vampire* c. 1894 and vampire lithographs 1895–1902. Similarly: Jules Laforgue passim, Rachilde *Monsieur Vénus* 1884 and "La buveuse de sang" 1900, Arthur Symons "The Vampire" *Lesbia* 1920, Stanislaw Przybyszewski *De profundis* 1895, Rudyard Kipling "The Vampire" 1897, Jean Lorrain *Monsieur de Phocas: Astarté* 1901—and, slurring both sides of sex, Maurice Rollinat "La chair" *Les névroses* 1883.

312. E.g., vampirism symbolized artistic creation in Jan Neruda "Vampyr" 1871, romantic poetry in Richard Dehmel "Bastard" 1893, and literary theft in George Sylvester Viereck *The House of the Vampire* 1907.

313. *The Death of Hippolytus* c. 1815.

314. *Hero Dies on Leander's Body* 1829.

315. Praz 114: c. 1851.

316. 1630–31; c. 1655; c. 1715–17. Fuseli's ghoulish *Death of Dido* 1781 was already a new departure.

317. 1851–52.

318. *The Death of Cleopatra* c. 1528; cf. Guido Reni c. 1626 and c. 1640–42, Alessandro Turchi 1635, Guido Cagnacci c. 1658–60, etc. But Guercino c. 1648 did lend his Cleopatra a faintly moribund air.

319. *The Death of Cleopatra* 1874–75; 1892—or, more discreetly, Arnold Böcklin 1878.

320. *Saint Agnes* 1635; *Young Martyr* c. 1650. The locus classicus of this look is Bernini's 1674 mortuary sculpture of the Blessed Lodovica Albertoni on the point of death.

321. E.g., Charles François Jalabert *The Young Martyr* 1855, Federico Faruffini *The Virgin on the Nile* 1865, Paul Delaroche *Young Martyr* 1855, Albert von Keller *In the Moonlight* 1894—and, in the male line, Armand Bloch's statue *The Martyr* 1891.

322. 1815–18.

323. From Charles Fournier *The Death of Abel* c. 1823 to Théodule Ribot *The Martyrdom of Saint Sebastian* 1865 and Jean Jacques Henner *Adam and Eve Discovering Abel's Body* 1868, *The Good Samaritan* 1874, and *The Death of Bara* 1882—plus, in sculpture, Giovanni Dupré *Dying Abel* 1842, Émile Feugère des Faits *Dead Abel* 1864, and Jean Marie Mangue *Icarus* 1887.

324. Clifford C. Olds in Levin 5.

325. *Paolo and Francesca* 1864.

326. *Paolo and Francesca* 1786; *Paolo and Francesca* 1819; *Paolo and Francesca* watercolor 1824–25; *Francesca da Rimini* 1837; *Paolo and Francesca* c. 1860–61; *Francesca da Rimini and Her Lover in the Park* c. 1875–80—and in sculpture Alexander Munro *Paolo and Francesca* 1851–52.

327. *Death of Francesca da Rimini and of Paolo Malatesta* 1870; cf. Ricardo Zandonai's opera *Francesca da Rimini* 1914, libretto by D'Annunzio.

328. 1855, recopied 1862.

329. *The Whirlwind of Lovers* c. 1824–26; *Paolo and Francesca* c. 1822 and 1854; *Francesca da Rimini* 1850; *Paolo and Francesca* 1872–84; *Paolo and Francesca* sculpture 1894; *Paolo and Francesca* 1893, 1895, and 1896; *Paolo and Francesca* 1901; *The Dream* 1908–9. Dante's illustrators included Blake, Delacroix, and Gustave Doré. On this nineteenth-century theme and variations see further Hartmann passim.

330. *Death of Romeo and Juliet* c. 1849–56; *The Reconciliation of the Montagues and Capulets* 1853–55; cf. Victor Müller *Romeo and Juliet* c. 1870.

331. *Romeo Lifting Juliet from the Capulet Tomb* c. 1851.

332. Chassériau *Last Encounter of Hero and Leander* 1849–56: Honour 308; cf. Turner *The Parting of Hero and Leander* 1837 with its magical affinity between the two fated figures. Already in William Etty *The Parting of Hero and Leander* 1827 and *Hero Dies on Leander's Body* 1829, Hero lay down with dead Leander as in Christopher Marlowe *Hero and Leander* 1593 (cf. n. 483): "She fell on her loves bosom, hugg'd it fast, / And with Leanders name she breath'd her last." Jean Joseph Taillasson's Leander of 1798 lay dead with open arms before a frantic Hero.

333. *Venus and Adonis* 1570–75; *The Death of Adonis in the Arms of Venus* c. 1612; Benjamin West *Venus Lamenting the Death of Adonis* c. 1763–67, 1768/ 1819, 1803.

334. *Cephalus and Procris* 1796; *Cephalus and Procris* 1817.

335. Fuseli *Criemhild Throwing Herself on Dead Siegfried* 1817.

336. Prud'hon *Phrosine and Mélidor* 1798.

337. Fuseli *Celadon and Amelia* 1801.

338. 1861; 1869; c. 1864 (poetized by Browning "Eurydice to Orpheus" 1864), numerous versions c. 1869.

339. Franz von Stuck *Orpheus* 1891; Aledár Kaziány *Orpheus* 1900, Gustave Moreau *Orpheus on Eurydice's Tomb* 1890.

340. Émile Lévy *The Death of Orpheus* 1866.

341. Gustave Moreau, countless versions 1865–98.

342. Jean Delville *Orpheus* 1893, Odilon Redon *Orpheus* c. 1903.

343. François Louis François *Orpheus* 1863.

344. Compare Pontormo 1529–30, Hendrick Goltzius engraving 1593, Matthäus Gundelach 1639, Jean Raoux 1717, Sebastiano Ricci c. 1717, François Le Moyne 1729, François Boucher c. 1750, Charles Eisen engravings c. 1750, and Étienne Maurice Falconet sculpture 1763 with Louis Lagrenée 1781, Alexandre Joseph Desenne engraving 1820, Octave Tassaert 1855, Edward Burne-Jones 1878, Auguste Rodin sculpture 1889, and Jean Léon Gérôme 1892. Matthäus Terwesten 1700–20 was betwixt and between.

345. Olds in Levin 5. In essence it was also a ritualized symbolic replay of the traumatic plague.

346. "Morte" *Iconologia* 1595.

347. Cohen passim, *Mâle* 222–27.

348. *La tentation de Saint Antoine* 1874.

349. Odilon Redon *White Female Body with Death's Head* lithograph 1888, *My Irony Exceeds All Others* lithograph 1889; numerous variants by Félicien Rops.

350. "Der Fischer" 1778, set to music by Johann Friedrich Reinhardt 1809, Franz Schubert 1815, Hector Berlioz in *Lelio ou le retour à la vie* 1830–31.

351. *The Rime of the Ancient Mariner* 1797–98; *Les Natchez* 1826: "Viens échanger des feux avec moi, et perdre la vie! mêlons des voluptés à la mort!"

352. "Amor e morte" 1832–33: "bellissima fanciulla."

353. *El diablo mundo* 1841.

354. "When Lilacs Last in the Dooryard Bloomed" 1865.

355. *Madame la Mort* 1891: Birkett 169.

356. "Tentation" *Au jardin de l'infante* 1893: "Viens, je suis la Mort douce, et l'amante attendue . . ."

357. *Lille Eyolf* 1894.

358. *Der Tod in Venedig* 1912.

359. But its prehistory goes back at least to Hades and Persephone, with numerous variants including Harlequin and Columbine: see McClelland 182–97.

360. Heine "Du schönes Fischermädchen" *Buch der Lieder* 1823; Schubert "Das Fischermädchen" *Schwanengesang*.

361. Further: Munch *The Kiss of Death* (lithograph) 1899. Death and the Maiden old-style meanwhile survived into Victor Hugo "Fantômes" 1828 and Louis Boulanger's corresponding lithograph *Les fantômes* 1829.

362. *El mágico prodigioso; Cardenio und Celinde*, both c. 1650.

363. *Traumbilder: V* 1817–21.

364. *El estudiante de Salamanca* 1840.

365. Praz 108 citing W. A. Reichart.

366. *Vij* 1835.

367. On her genealogy and metamorphoses see Praz 139–212 ("La Belle Dame Sans Merci"). Praz missed Eichendorff's bewitching "Lorelei" in *Ahnung*

und Gegenwart 1811/15 and the "eternal courtesan" serving Satan in Gérard de Nerval *L'imagier de Harlem* 1851.

368. E.g., "Laus Veneris," "Faustine," "The Masque of Queen Bersabe" all 1865: Praz 173–78.

369. E.g., *Helen of Troy* 1863, *Venus Verticordia* 1864, *Lady Lilith* 1868, *The Bower Meadow* and *Proserpine* 1872, *A Sea-Spell* and *The Blessed Damozel* 1877, *The Daydream* 1880; cf. Rossetti's corresponding poems "The Blessed Damozel" 1841 and "Lilith" 1869.

370. *Isis* 1862. In Catulle Mendès *La première maîtresse* 1887 a mature woman preys on virgin boys this same way.

371. "Les yeux glauques" *Buveurs d'âmes* 1893: Birkett 197.

372. Praz 189–208 on D'Annunzio's *Poema paradisiaco* 1893, *Il fuoco* 1893, and esp. *Il trionfo della morte* 1894.

373. Vetter 129–75 ("Die femme fatale") sees a native touch to only the Jugendstil nixie.

374. *The Depths of the Sea* 1887.

375. *The Bride of the Night* c. 1892.

376. *Caresses* 1896.

377. *Nude Redhead* c. 1910.

378. "Dalila" *L'illusion* 1875: "Et comment, femme, . . . toi qui donnes la vie, es-tu pleine de mort?"

379. *Sin* 1893, *Sensuality* prints 1889–97. Fuseli had already stressed her compliant affinity with death: *Sin Pursued by Death* 1794–96.

380. "Die Spinne" 1908.

381. "Der Schatten" 1913.

382. 1893–94 (Munch quoted by Eggum 166).

383. *Alraune* 1911. For further overlaps see Comini passim, Kingsbury passim.

384. But in Conrad Meit's statue *Judith* c. 1525–28 she holds the severed head by the hair, gazing at it almost tenderly (cf. n. 389 below). And in one of Bernardo Cavallino's episodes of her story she rests her hand on a shawl over the severed head while smiling for the painter: c. 1650.

385. Choice examples are Hans Baldung Grien 1525, Jan Massys 1543, and Jan Sanders van Hemessen c. 1549–50.

386. 1917; 1901; 1898/1907.

387. 1909.

388. See especially Francesco del Cairo's several versions c. 1650.

389. But in a Bernardo Strozzi of the early 1630s Salome wistfully fondles a lock of the Baptist's hair (cf. n. 384 above).

390. *The Daughter of Herodias with the Head of Saint John the Baptist* c. 1779 (engraving).

391. "Hérodias" 1877, *Salomé* 1891; *Hérodias* 1881, *Salome* (print) 1905; 1876; 1905. For numberless examples see Daffner 298–388, Reimarus Secundus III 101–93, Praz 216–28, Dijkstra 379–401. To go by the Talmud, Salome had a necrophiliac heritage in that Herod the Great, her stepfather's father, who was also both her father's father and her mother's paternal grandfather, continued to sleep with his first wife for seven years after she was murdered.

392. Tintner 129–35.

393. *Don Juan* 1919–24. Cf. the stagy villain in Lajos Gulácsy's *Don Juan's Garden* 1910.

394. Francesco Maffei *Perseus and Medusa* early 1650s is a notable exception. (Lone severed Medusa heads were less rare; a gripping one was Lévy-Dhurmer's pastel of 1897.)

395. *David and the Head of Goliath* c. 1715—probably a self-portrait. David's few modern appearances with Goliath's head are traditional, as in statues by Edo Kallós 1892 and Zsigmond Kisfaludy Strobl 1912.

396. See, e.g., Lucas Cranach woodcut c. 1501–4, Albrecht Dürer etching 1504–5, Luca Cambiaso drawings c. 1550–80, Marco d'Oggiono 1520s, Giovanni Lanfranco c. 1605, Cristofano Allori(?) 1606–10, Pier Francesco Morazzone c. 1611, Guido Cagnacci c. 1640, Lieven Mehus c. 1660.

397. She might even hold his bleeding body alone while his mother prayed, as in Juan de Juanes 1550–75.

398. Pierre Juste Sautel *Divae Magdalenae ignes sacri et piae lacrymae* 1656.

399. Frontrunners include Titian c. 1531–35, Sodoma(?) c. 1540s, Cornelis Cornelisz Van Haarlem 1608, Alessandro Allori c. 1610, Christoph Helfenrieder c. 1630, Giovanni Cantarini(?) c. 1630, Sigismondo Coccapani c. 1635, Guido Cagnacci c. 1640, Simone Pignoni (Furini's pupil) c. 1640–60, Gerrit Dou 1660s, Elisabetta Sirani 1663, Gian Giuseffo dal Sole c. 1700, and Adriaen Van der Werff c. 1710. A mid–seventeenth-century trompe-l'oeil by Matteo Rosselli shows her and Jesus two-in-one.

400. *Agony* 1901; *Mary Magdalen Mourning the Dead Christ* 1867–68 (imitated by Ludwig von Löfftz *Lamentation of Christ by the Magdalen* 1883); François Xavier Fabre 1805, Jean Baptiste Maes-Canini c. 1822, Francesco Hayez 1825, Paul Baudry 1859, Jean Jacques Henner c. 1874, Jules Joseph Lefèbvre 1876, Marius Vasselon 1887, Adolphe La Lyre 1892, Jean Béraud 1907.

401. "Je n'ai pas pour maîtresse . . ." c. 1840: "Je la lèche en silence avec plus de ferveur / Que Madeleine en feu les deux pieds du Sauveur."

402. "Mary Magdalen at the Door of Simon the Pharisee" 1870.

403. *Christ's Lover* 1887.

404. *Christ and the Magdalen* c. 1894; *Deposition* 1895.

405. Thus Pisanello's ink drawing of hanged men for his fresco *San Giorgio e la principessa* 1433–38.

406. Gauguin seems to have parodied this practice in *Breton Calvary: Green Christ* 1889 and *Yellow Christ* 1889.

407. *Pietà* c. 1470; *The Corpse of Christ Held by Angels* and *Pietà* c. 1475; *Dead Christ* c. 1490.

408. *Descent from the Cross* c. 1500; *Deposition* 1517, *Dead Christ with Angels* c. 1526, and *Pietà* 1530–35.

409. *Crucifixion* c. 1515; *Pietà* 1519.

410. *Dead Christ* 1521; *Lamentation* c. 1527.

411. *The Lamentation* c. 1523–24; *Pietà* c. 1530.

412. *Pietà* 1535–40; *Pietà* several versions c. 1553–70.

413. *Dead Christ* c. 1606; *Dead Christ* sculpture 1614; *Christ in the Sepulcher* c. 1617–19. Paul Troger *Annointing of Christ's Corpse* c. 1730–38 is still grim.

414. Dead Jesus writhed with his head between an ecstatic Mary's legs in a Jacques Bellange etching of 1615 after a lost Michelangelo relief.

415. Giuseppe Sammartino 1753—based, however, on a deathly model by Antonio Corradini 1752.

416. Raimundus da Capua *Vita* c. 1385–95; her discussion in her *Dialogus* of Christ's words "Come to me and drink" looks watered down beside this episode as told by her confessor. Thereafter she could eat and drink only the sacramental bread and wine; as the Lord explained to her in her dialogue, "You may have life by receiving His body in food and His blood in drink."

417. Quoted Pfister 47–48; further, ibid. 47–68 on Zinzendorf's orgasmic cult of the dead Christ's blood, sweat, pus, defunct member, and feminized gashes (all presented wrongly as Zinzendorf's personal pathology).

418. *Crucifixion* 1822; *Pietà* 1842; *Entombment* 1834, *Crucifixion* 1835, 1846, 1853, c. 1853–56, *Pietà* 1844, c. 1850, *Lamentation* 1848, 1849, 1853; *The Dead Christ* 1874; *Lamentation* 1876; *Jesus in the Tomb* 1879, *The Dead Christ* 1896; *Pietà* 1891; *Dead Christ Mourned by Holy Women* 1893.

419. Above, n. 107. Similarly in Villiers de l'Isle-Adam "L'amour suprême" 1886 the heroine's sex appeal soars as, shrouded, she steps into a Carmelite coffin: Birkett 30.

420. Praz 127–28 and n. 167.

421. *Le calvaire* 1887; "L'adorant" 1896; *La cathédrale* 1898 (where she is dubbed the "Virgin of the Crypt"): Birkett 238, 104, 95–97.

422. *L'abbé Jules* 1888: Birkett 244 (retranslated).

423. *Temptation* 1878—a takeoff on Flaubert. Similarly Norman Lindsay *The Crucified Venus* drawing 1912.

424. *Sébastien Roch* 1890: Birkett 241–42 (retranslated). Cf. Steinberg pp. 317–18 on the American feminization of Jesus 1840–1910.

425. *Le fantôme* 1891: Birkett 112 (retranslated).

426. *Là-bas* 1891: Birkett 89. Cf. Angela of Foligno, who in the 1290s stripped and offered herself to a Christ naked on the cross ("expoliavi me omnia vestimenta mea et totam me obtuli ei": Thier and Calufetti 136), then kissed him back to life and love in his tomb ("et postea osculata est os eius . . .": ibid. 296, cf. 136).

427. "Sur un Dieu mort" *Buveurs d'âmes* 1893: Birkett 89.

428. *Pollice verso* 1904.

429. Karl Hans Strobl "Das Aderlaßmännchen" 1909: Vetter 19.

430. *Neue Gedichte*: "Wir legten uns noch nie zusammen nieder, / . . . / Wie gehn wir beide wunderlich zugrund."

431. Herbert Eulenberg "Der alte Schäfer" *Sonderbare Geschichten* 1916.

432. "Rede des todten Christus vom Weltgebäude herab, daß kein Gott sei" 1795.

433. *Die Leiden des jungen Werther* 1774; *Ultime lettere di Jacopo Ortiz* 1798–1802; *Hymnen an die Nacht* 1800.

434. "Mein süßes Lieb" *Lyrisches Intermezzo* 1827.

435. 1827. Similarly in Beddoes's posthumous fragment *The Second Brother*: "I love no ghost. I loved the fairest woman."

436. "Véra" 1874–80. Both parties to the love-death in Villiers's posthumous *Axël* denied "the Light, the Hope, and the Life."

437. 1900.

438. [Évariste Boulay-Paty] *Élie Mariaker* 1834: "J'interroge un cadavre, une main sur son coeur."

439. "Prisraki" 1863.

440. "Les tombales" 1891.

441. "La tombe" 1884; similarly "La morte" 1887 on a beloved's incomprehensible goneness. On the pervasiveness of death in Maupassant's prose: Buisine passim.

442. To George Sand late September 1866 ("J'ai rêvé et très peu exécuté"): quoted Maigron 175n.

443. "An Helios" 1814.

444. Proelß 249.

445. *Mors Janua Vitae* 1905–9: Darment 43–46.

446. Dijkstra 45, 51–53, 348; above, n. 75.

447. Praz 299. Not just the decadent woman, but "for a time the romantic woman affected a pale, livid, spectral look": Maigron 182.

448. Spring 1802. (She did commit suicide four years later, though over another lover.)

449. To Fanny Brawne 25 July 1819.

450. To Lord Alfred Douglas summer 1894: Ellmann 408.

451. Letter of 27 March 1853: Praz 22, further 132 n. 78.

452. *Mes cahiers*: August 1901.

453. Maigron 176, Praz 96.

454. *Journal* 18 December 1860.

455. Binion *Soundings* 62–63 and n. 5.

456. By all accounts he was condemned in 1848 or 1849 to the maximum penalty of a year's imprisonment, but no such sentence was registered under the apposite rubric ("violations de sépulture") for the years 1847 through 1850: *Compte-Rendu Général de l'Administration de la Justice Criminelle en France* (annual: Paris 1848–51).

457. Praz 234; *Là-bas* 1891.

458. Locus classicus: Jacques Peuchet *Mémoires tirés des archives de la police de Paris pour servir à l'histoire de la morale et de la police* (1838) I: 144–60.

459. The best was Alexis Épaulard *Vampirisme: Nécrophilie, nécrosadisme, nécrophagie* 1901.

460. The best known were Léo Taxil *La prostitution contemporaine: Étude d'une question sociale* (1884) 171 and *La corruption fin de siècle* (1894) 242–43—likely sources for Jean Genet *Le balcon*.

461. Ariès *Essais* 177–210; Mitchell 688–91; Vovelle 698–709.

462. *Le spéronare* 1842; *La vie errante* 1903.

463. Cf. above, nn. 207, 208, and 441. Further, Maupassant "Les tombales" 1891: "Poor darling, she was so nice and loving, so white, so fresh . . . and now . . . if that were opened . . ."

464. "Bist du nun tot?" *Der ewige Tag* 1911: "Bist du das, was ich einst so heiß umschlang?"

465. "La morte embaumée," "La bière," "L'ensevelissement," "Ballade du cadavre," "La putréfaction" *Les névroses* 1883.

466. c. 1892.

467. Linse passim.

468. "In morte di Madonna Laura" by 1362: "Quanta invidia io ti porto, avara terra, / Ch'abbracci quella cui veder m'è tolto . . ."

469. "E mi contendi l'aria del bel volto / Dove pace trovai d'ogni mia guerra!"

470. "Torno a veder ond'al ciel nuda è gita / Lasciando in terra la sua bella spoglia."

471. *Della Tersicore, ovvero scherzi e paradossi sopra la beltà delle donne fra' difetti ancora ammirabili e vaghe* 1637: "Per esser come tè bella nel fine / Se potesse morir, morria la Morte."

472. Praz 5.

473. More nearly necrophiliac was the rash of Neapolitan sonnets in 1590 for Maria d'Avales, slain with her lover by an irate husband: "or giaccion morti abbracciati . . ." ran one by Giovan Battista Marino (Borzelli 301).

474. Abbé Prévost *Histoire du chevalier des Grieux et de Manon Lescaut* 1731.

475. "Lamia" 1819. (Elisabeth's "bridal bier" in Mary Shelley's *Frankenstein* may have inspired that twist.)

476. Cf. n. 216.

477. *Doctor Faustus* c. 1588. In the Faust Book, Marlowe's source, he had a child by her, then both vanished when he died.

478. *Der Doktor Faust: Ein Tanzpoem* 1851: "Du hast mich beschworen aus dem Grab / Durch deinen Zauberwillen, / Belebtest mich mit Wollustglut— / Jetzt kannst du die Glut nicht stillen. / Preß deinen Mund an meinen Mund. / Der Menschen Odem ist göttlich! / Ich trinke deine Seele aus. / Die Toten sind unersättlich."

479. Daffner 72–74.

480. *Death as a Warrior Embraces a Young Woman.*

481. Sophocles *Antigone* 899.

482. Cf. Antigone in Aeschylus *Seven against Thebes* 1040: "myself will shroud him" (her slain brother).

483. Perhaps already in the 1590s with Marlowe's *Hero and Leander* (cf. n. 332) and *Doctor Faustus* or Shakespeare's *Richard III* and *Romeo and Juliet*. But a Shakespeare cried "for restful death" only to add: "Save that, to die, I leave my love alone" (Sonnet LXVI), whereas a Keats would not double back on his Fanny's account in musing: "Now more than ever seems it rich to die" ("Ode to a Nightingale" 1819).

484. "The Funerall," "The Relique," "The Apparition" 1633.

485. "Farewell to Love" 1650.

486. Summers 308–10.

487. See above, n. 391.

488. *L'Atlantide.*

489. *Orphée* 1926, film 1949.

490. *Eurydice* 1942.

491. *Orpheus Descending* 1957. The Franco-Italo-Brazilian film *Black Orpheus* 1958 followed in this line.

492. *Judith* 1931.

493. 1930.

494. *Histoire de l'oeil* 1928; *Le bleu du ciel* 1934.

495. Albert Cohen *Belle du Seigneur* 1968.

496. *Pietà* 1920; *Jesus Christ Offering Us His Blood* 1925; *Pietà* 1929.

497. But Rouault repeated his stylized crucifixion of 1913 stereotypically in 1918, then 1930, 1935, and 1939.

498. *Jonk the Killer* drawing 1916, *John the Ladies' Murderer* 1918; *The Sex Murderer* 1917; *Night* 1918–19; *The Sex Murderer (Self-Portrait)* 1920, *Sex Murder* 1922. Further, Frida Kahlo *A Few Small Pricks* 1935.

499. Arturo Martini *Ophelia* sculpture 1933; Salomé *Judith and Holofernes* 1981; Margit Kovács *Salome* sculpture 1943–44; Hans Pontiker *Salome* sculpture 1958, Györgyi Lantos *Salome* sculpture 1985.

500. Hartmann 24.

501. E.g., Alfred Kubin *Die Blätter mit dem Tod* 1918, Gabriele Gabrielli *The Cavalcade of Death* c. 1918, José Gotiérrez Solana *The End of the World* c. 1932, Otto Dix *The Seven Deadly Sins* 1933, Käthe Kollwitz *Death* lithograph series 1934–37, Peter Sellemond *Dance of Death* sculpture 1936, Paul Delvaux *The Spitzner Museum* 1943, *The Red City* 1943–44, *Sleeping Venus*, and *Conversation* 1944. Literarily, if Cocteau for one retained "Madame la Mort" in *Orphée*, the title character of Agatha Christie's *The Mysterious Mr. Quin* 1930 was death himself in the guise of an amiable lover.

502. Hessisches Landesmuseum 68–85 ("Tod und Erotik").

503. Zentralinstitut für Sepulkralkultur Nos. 47, 58, 60, and passim. In Italian parlance, however, death remains "la terribile signora."

504. *Kádár Kata* 1962.

505. "Die lädierte Welt" exhibit, Kunstforum Länderbank, Vienna, 1987: Adolf Frohner *The Youngsters in the Oven* 1986, *The Long Wait* 1979, *Cain and Abel Dance* 1986; Rainer Wölzl *Skin* 1986, *Two Figures II* 1986, *Two Figures III* 1986; Alfred Hrdlicka *The Death of Marat* 1987.

506. Catherine L. Moore "Shambleau" 1953. No items shown in the 1987 exhibit "Zauber der Medusa" held in Vienna's Künstlerhaus postdated 1919.

507. *Green Arrow* (comic book) 17 April 1989, cover and p. 23: "No ID . . ."

508. "Hollywood's definition of a perfect couple is a man and a woman, one of whom is dead": David Ansen in *Newsweek* 16 July 1990, 61. That perfect couple comes apart domestically in Anthony Minghella's 1991 British screen comedy *Truly, Madly, Deeply*.

509. *Dick Tracy* 1990.

510. One had merit: Werner Herzog's 1978 remake of *Nosferatu*.

511. Perhaps its highest note was struck on the screen in *Looking for Mr. Goodbar* 1977.

512. *Les loukoums* 1973; *Song of Solomon* 1977; cf. Camilo José Cela *Mrs. Caldwell habla con su hijo* 1953, with its mother's mad love for a dead son, and Felisberto Hernández "Las hortensias" 1966, on an inflated mannequin substituted for a wife. I could not run down Nelly Kaplan *Le plaisir solidaire*, reportedly a woman's account of her joyous resuscitation by a necrophile.

513. *Le balcon* 1957; *Belle de jour* 1968.

514. *Taxi Driver* 1976; Terry 58–60 and passim.

515. Bugliosi 56 and passim. Terry 613 and passim: rape-and-murder is stock ritual with satanic cults.

516. Or not even: in the video series *Faces of Death* the "snuff" footage is reputedly bogus.

517. Less so early Greek beliefs: Vermeule 54–56, Keuls 129–32.

518. Hirschfeld 522; Thomas passim.

519. On this and the next three sentences: Hertz passim; Huntington and Metcalf 98–118, 179; Bloch and Parry 1–44, 221. Cf. in Western fantasy Bernardo Bertolucci's film about a fit of erotomania attending a wife's death, *Last Tango in Paris* (1972), or at a psychotic extreme Norman Mailer's novel of sexual emancipation through a wife murder, *An American Dream* (1965).

520. Cf. the equivalence of winding sheets with swaddling clothes in premodern practice in the West; cf. Margit Kovács *Death* 1968. Neanderthals already buried their dead in foetal posture.

521. Binion *Frau Lou* 382n, 384–85.

522. See especially Mario Praz and Gershon Legman passim.

523. Binion *After Christianity* 120–22 and passim.

524. "Aubade" 1977. Further: "This is a special way of being afraid / No trick dispels. Religion used to try, / That vast moth-eaten musical brocade / Created to pretend we never die."

525. Gershon Legman made this point compellingly already in 1949.

526. E.g. (to sample just America), *The Invasion of the Body Snatchers* 1966, *The Night of the Living Dead* 1968, *Deathdream* 1972, *The Texas Chainsaw Massacre* 1974, *Halloween* 1978 and 1981, *Friday the Thirteenth* 1980, 1981, and 1982, *The Silence of the Lambs* 1991.

527. Slayer "Necrophobic" *Reign in Blood* 1986.

528. Larry Clark *Tulsa* 1971, *Teenage Lust* 1983.

529. "Mercy" *Taboo* II (1989) 108–14—possibly inspired by Martin Scorsese's 1988 film *The Last Temptation of Christ*.

530. Binion *After Christianity* 21–68.

Locations of Art Works Cited

(excluding prints)

ALEXANDER John White *Isabella and the Pot of Basil* 1897 Boston: Museum of Fine Arts.

ALLORI Alessandro *Magdalen Seated in the Desert* c. 1610 Florence: Galleria Palatina.

ALLORI Cristofano(?) *The Magdalen Transported by Angels* 1606–10 Pistoia: San Domenico.

ASPERTINI Amico *Pietà* 1519 Bologna: San Petronio.

BALDUNG GRIEN Hans *Judith* 1525 Nuremberg: Germanisches National-museum. *Lamentation* c. 1527 Berlin-Dahlem: Gemäldegalerie.

BARRY James *King Lear Weeping over the Dead Body of Cordelia* 1786–87 London: Tate Gallery.

BARTOLO Taddeo *Last Judgment* 1393 San Gimignano: Collegiata.

BARTOLOMEO DA VENEZIA *Female Half Figure* c. 1520–25 Frankfurt: Städelsches Kunstinstitut.

BAUDRY Paul *Zenobia Found by Shepherds* 1850 Paris: École des Beaux-Arts. *Penitent Magdalen* 1859 Nantes: Musée des Beaux-Arts.

BECKMANN Max *Big Death Scene* 1905 Munich: Haus der Kunst. *Night* 1918–19 Düsseldorf: Kunstsammlung Nordrhein-Westfalen.

BEEKS Jan Van *Long Live Death* 1873 Brussels: Musées Royaux des Beaux-Arts.

BELLINI Giovanni *Pietà* c. 1470 Milan: Brera.

BÉRAUD Jean *Mary Magdalen* 1907 Troyes: Musée des Beaux-Arts.

BERNHARDT Sarah *Ophelia* c. 1881 lost (survives in photographs).

BERNINI Giovanni Lorenzo *The Blessed Lodovica Albertoni* 1674 Rome: San Francesco a Ripa.

BERTRAND James Jean Baptiste *Ophelia's Death* 1872 sold London: Sotheby's Belgravia 1979.

BLAKE William *The Whirlwind of Lovers* c. 1824–26 Birmingham: City Museum and Art Gallery.

BLOCH Armand *The Martyr* 1891 Paris: Musée d'Orsay.

BOCCIONI Umberto *The Dream* 1908–9 private collection.

BÖCKLIN Arnold *Mary Magdalen Mourning the Dead Christ* 1867–68 Basel: Kunstmuseum. *Francesca da Rimini and Her Lover in the Park* c. 1875–80 Darmstadt: Hessisches Landesmuseum. *Lamentation* 1876 Berlin: Nationalgalerie. *The Death of Cleopatra* 1878 Basel: Kunstmuseum. *Dead Girl's Head* 1879 Basel: Kunstmuseum. *Paolo and Francesca* 1893 Winterthur: Stiftung Oskar Reinhart, 1895 Weimar: Staatliche Kunstsammlungen, 1896 lost.

BONNARD Pierre *Woman Dozing on a Bed* 1899 Paris: Musée d'Orsay.

BOUCHER François *Pygmalion* c. 1750 Leningrad: Hermitage.

BOUGUEREAU William Adolphe *Zenobia Found by Shepherds* 1850 Paris: École des Beaux-Arts.

BOURDELLE Émile Antoine *Tragedy* 1912 Paris: Musée Bourdelle.

BROC Jean *Death of Hyacinth* 1801 Poitiers: Musée de la Ville de Poitiers.

BRONZINO Agnolo *Pietà* c. 1530 Florence: Uffizi.

BROOKS Romaine *Le trajet* c. 1911 Washington, D.C.: Smithsonian Institution.

BUFFET Bernard *Pietà* 1946 Vatican: Museo di Arte Moderna.

BURNE-JONES Edward *The Sleeping Princess* 1873–90 Buscot Park, Berkshire: Faringdon Collection Trust. *Pygmalion and the Image* 1878 Birmingham: Birmingham Museum and Art Gallery. *The Depths of the Sea* 1887 Cambridge (Massachusetts): Fogg Museum of Art.

BURNE-JONES Philip *The Vampire* 1897 location unknown.

CABANEL Alexandre *Death of Francesca da Rimini and of Paolo Malatesta* 1870 Paris: Musée d'Orsay.

CAGNACCI Guido *The Magdalen Transported to Heaven* c. 1640 Florence: Palazzo Pitti. *Young Martyr* c. 1650 Montpellier: Musée Fabre. *The Death of Cleopatra* c. 1658–60 Vienna: Kunsthistorisches Museum, Bologna: Palazzo d'Accursio.

CAIRO Francesco del *Saint Agnes* 1635 Turin: Galleria Sabauda. *Herodias with the Head of John the Baptist* c. 1650 Boston: Museum of Fine Arts, Vicenza: Palazzo Chiericati, Turin: Galleria Sabauda.

CALLOT Georges *The Death of the Little Courtesan* 1901 lost.

CAMBIASO Luca *Venus and Adonis* 1570–75 Leningrad: Hermitage, Rome: Galleria d'Arte Antica. *The Magdalen Transported to Heaven* c. 1550 Paris: Musée du Louvre, c. 1560 Florence: Uffizi, c. 1570 and c. 1580 London: Victoria and Albert Museum.

CANOVA Antonio *Cephalus and Procris* 1796 Possagno: Gipsoteca.

CANTARINI Giovanni (?) *The Magdalen* c. 1630 Venice: Querini-Stampaglia.

CARRACCI Annibale *Dead Christ* c. 1606 Stuttgart: Staatsgalerie.

CAVALLINO Bernardo *Judith and the Head of Holofernes* c. 1650 Stockholm: Statens Konstmuseer.

CELLINI Benvenuto *Perseus* 1545–54 Florence: Loggia dei Lanzi.

CHAGALL Marc *White Crucifixion* 1938 Chicago: Art Institute.

CHASSÉRIAU Théodore *Death of Romeo and Juliet* c. 1849–56 Paris: Musée du Louvre. *Last Encounter of Hero and Leander* 1849–56 Paris: Musée du Louvre.

CIAMBERLANI Albert *Ophelia* by 1900 Brussels: Musées Royaux des Beaux-Arts.

CLÉSINGER Auguste *Woman Bitten by a Snake* 1847 Paris: Musée d'Orsay.

COCCAPANI Sigismondo *The Magdalen in Ecstasy* c. 1635 Besançon: Musée des Beaux-Arts, Florence: Depositi del Palazzo Pitti.

CORINTH Lovis *Deposition* 1895 [Berlin: Dr. B. von Dernburg 1925].

CORNELISZ VAN HARRLEM Cornelis *Mary Magdalen* 1608 sold London: Sotheby's 17 May 1961.

COROT Camille *Orphée* 1861 Switzerland: private collection.

CORRADINI Antonio *Dead Christ* 1752 Berlin: Staatliche Museen Stiftung Preußischer Kulturbesitz, Skulpturgalerie.

CORREGGIO *The Lamentation* c. 1523–24 Parma: Galleria Nazionale.

COYPEL Antoine *The Death of Dido* c. 1715–17 Montpellier: Musée Fabre.

CRANACH Lucas the Elder *Judith* c. 1530 Prague: Národní Galerie.

DALI Salvador *Christ of Saint John of the Cross* 1951 Glasgow: Glasgow Art Gallery and Museum.

DAVID Jacques Louis *Figure académique* c. 1820 Paris: Musée du Louvre.

DAVRINGHAUSEN Heinrich *The Sex Murderer* 1917 Munich: Haus der Kunst.

DELACROIX Eugène *Paolo and Francesca* watercolor 1824–25 Zurich: Peter Nathan. *The Death of Sardanapalus* 1827 Paris: Musée du Louvre. *Entombment* 1834 Cairo: Mahmoud Khalil Museum. *Crucifixion* 1835 Vannes: Musée Municipal des Beaux-Arts, 1846 Baltimore: Walters Art Gallery, 1853: London: National Gallery, c. 1853–56 Bremen: Kunsthalle. *The Death of Ophelia* 1838 Munich: Neue Pinakothek, 1844 Winterthur: Oskar Reinhart, 1853 (drawing and painting) Paris: Musée du Louvre. *Pietà* 1844 Paris: Musée du

Louvre, c. 1850 Oslo: Nasjonalgalleriet. *Odalisque* c. 1845–50 Cambridge: Fitzwilliam Museum. *Lamentation* 1848 Boston: Museum of Fine Arts, 1849 Phoenix: Art Museum, 1853 Zurich: Peter Nathan. *Apollo Triumphant* c. 1851 Paris: Musée du Louvre (Apollo Gallery). *Romeo Lifting Juliet from the Capulet Tomb* c. 1851 lost (survives in lithographs).

DELAROCHE Paul *The Young Martyr* 1855 Paris: Musée du Louvre.

DELVAUX Paul *The Spitzner Museum* 1943 private collection. *The Red City* 1943–44 Rotterdam: Museum Boymans-Van Beuningen. *Sleeping Venus* 1944 London: Tate Gallery. *Conversation* 1944 New York: Peter A. de Maerel.

DELVILLE Jean *Tristan and Isolt* 1887 Brussels: Musées Royaux des Beaux-Arts. *Orpheus* 1893 Brussels: Anne-Marie Gillion Crowet. *Satan's Treasures* 1895 Brussels: Musées Royaux des Beaux-Arts. *Love of Souls* 1900 Brussels: Musée d'Ixelles.

DILLENS Julien *Figure for a Tomb* 1887 Brussels: Musées Royaux des Beaux-Arts.

DIX Otto *The Sex Murderer (Self-Portrait)* 1920: location unknown. *Sex Murder* 1922 Stuttgart: private collection. *Still Life in the Studio* 1924 Stuttgart: Galerie der Stadt Stuttgart. *The Seven Deadly Sins* 1933 Karlsruhe: Staatliche Kunsthalle.

DONATELLO *David* c. 1430 Florence: Museo Nazionale del Bargello.

DOU Gerrit *The Penitent Magdalen* 1660s Karlsruhe: Kunsthalle.

DRAPER Herbert James *The Lament for Icarus* 1898 London: Tate Gallery.

DUPRÉ Giovanni *Dying Abel* 1842.

DYCE William *Francesca da Rimini* 1837 Edinburgh: National Gallery of Scotland.

ETTY William *The Parting of Hero and Leander* 1827 London: Tate Gallery. *Hero Dies on Leander's Body* 1829 York: City Art Gallery.

FABRE François Xavier *Mary Magdalen* 1805 Montpellier: Musée Fabre.

FALCONET Étienne Maurice *Pygmalion* 1763 Baltimore: Walters Art Gallery.

FARUFFINI Federico *The Virgin on the Nile* 1865 Rome: Galleria Nazionale d'Arte Moderna.

FERNÁNDEZ Gregorio *Dead Christ* 1614 El Pardo: Monasterío Capuchino.

FEUERBACH Anselm *Paolo and Francesca* 1864 Munich: Bayerische Staatsgemäldesammlungen. *Orpheus and Eurydice* 1869 Vienna: Kunsthistorisches Museum.

FEUGÈRE DES FORTS Émile *Dead Abel* 1864 Paris: Musée d'Orsay.

FLANDRIN Hippolyte *Pietà* 1842 Lyons: Musée des Beaux-Arts.

FLAUN Franz *Vampire* c. 1904 lost.

FORD Edward Onslow *Shelley Memorial* 1891 Oxford: University College.

FOULD Consuelo *Buried Alive* 1898 lost.

FOURNIER Charles *The Death of Abel* c. 1823 Paris: Musée du Louvre.

FRANÇAIS François Louis *Orpheus* 1863 Paris: Musée d'Orsay.

FRANCESCHI Emilio *Eulalia christiana* 1887 Turin: Civica Galleria d'Arte Moderna.

FRASCHIERI Giuseppe *Francesca da Rimini* 1850 Genoa-Narvi: Civica Galleria d'Arte Moderna.

FURINI Francesco *Penitent Magdalen* c. 1630 Vienna: Kunsthistorisches Museum, c. 1633 Florence: Emilio Pucci, c. 1635 Stuttgart: Staatsgalerie.

FUSELI Henry *Death of Dido* 1781 sold Richard L. Feigen 1974. *Paolo and Francesca* 1786 Aarau: Argauer Kunsthaus. *Sin Pursued by Death* 1794–96 Zurich: Kunsthaus. *Celadon and Amelia* 1801 Karlsruhe: Staatliches Kunsthaus. *Romeo at Juliet's Bier* 1809 Basel: private collection. *Wolfram Watching His Wife in Her Cell* c. 1815 Nuremberg: Germanisches Nationalmuseum. *Criemhild Throwing Herself on Dead Siegfried* 1817 Zurich: Kunsthaus.

GABRIELLI Gabriele *The Cavalcade of Death* c. 1918 Livorno: Museo Civico Fattori.

GAUGUIN Paul *Yellow Christ* 1889 Buffalo: Albright-Knox Art Gallery. *Breton Calvary: Green Christ* 1889 Brussels: Musées Royaux des Beaux-Arts.

GÉRICAULT Jean Louis André Théodore copy of figure from Prud'hon *Justice and Divine Retribution Pursuing Crime* c. 1812 Paris: Musée du Louvre. *The Death of Hippolytus* c. 1815 Montpellier: Musée Fabre.

GÉRÔME Jean Léon *Pygmalion and Galatea* 1892 New York: Metropolitan Museum of Art.

GIGOUX Jean François *The Death of Cleopatra* 1892 Chambéry: Musée des Beaux-Arts.

GILBERT Alfred *The Enchanted Chair* 1886 destroyed. *Mors Janua Vitae* 1905–9 London: Royal College of Surgeons of England.

GIRARDI Fabio *Cephalus and Procris* c. 1817 Venice: Accademia.

GIRODET DE ROUCY-TRIOSON Anne Louis *The Sleep of Endymion* 1793 Paris: Musée du Louvre. *Atala's Burial* 1808 Paris: Musée du Louvre.

GROSZ George *Jonk the Killer* 1916 Princeton: estate of George Grosz. *John the Ladies' Murderer* 1918 Hamburg: Kunsthalle.

GRÜNEWALD Matthias *Crucifixion* c. 1515 Colmar: Musée Unterlinden.

GUERCINO *The Death of Dido* 1630–31 Rome: Galleria Spada. *The Death of Cleopatra* c. 1648 Genoa: Palazzo Rosso.

GUÉRIN Pierre Narcisse *Aurora and Cephalus* 1810 Paris: Musée du Louvre, 1811 Leningrad: Hermitage.

GULÁCSY Lajos *Don Juan's Garden* 1910 Budapest: Nemzeti Múzeum.

GUNDELACH Matthäus *Venus in Pygmalion's Workshop* 1639 Kassel: Staatliche Kunstsammlungen.

HAYEZ Francesco *The Penitent Magdalen* 1825 Milan: private collection.

HÉBERT Pierre Eugène Émile *Et toujours! Et jamais!* 1859/63 Lawrence (Kansas): Spencer Museum of Art.

HELFENRIEDER Christoph *Saint Mary Magdalen* c. 1630 Innsbruck: Ferdinandeum.

HEMESSEN Jan Sanders Van *Judith with the Head of Holofernes* c. 1549–50 Chicago: Art Institute.

HENNER Jean Jacques *Adam and Eve Discovering Abel's Body* 1868 Paris: École des Beaux-Arts. *The Good Samaritan* 1874 Montpellier: Musée Fabre. *The Magdalen Kneeling in the Grotto* c. 1874 Paris: Musée du Petit Palais. *Jesus in the Tomb* 1879 Paris: Musée d'Orsay. *The Death of Bara* 1882 Paris: Musée du Louvre. *The Dead Christ* 1896 Lyons: Musée Municipal. *The Levite of Ephraim and His Dead Wife* 1898 sold New York: Sotheby's Parke-Bernet 25 April 1985.

HOLBEIN Hans *Dead Christ* 1521 Basel: Kunstmuseum.

HUNT William Holman *Isabella and the Pot of Basil* 1866–68/1886 Newcastle-upon-Tyne: Laing Art Gallery.

INGRES Jean Auguste Dominique *Paolo and Francesca* 1819 Angers: Musée Pincé.

JALABERT Charles François *The Young Martyr* 1855 Baltimore: Walters Art Gallery.

JUANES Juan de *Pietà* 1550–75 Dallas: Southern Methodist University.

KAHLO Frida *A Few Small Pricks* 1935 Mexico City: La Noria.

KALLÓS Ede *David* 1892 Budapest: Nemzeti Múzeum.

KAZIÁNY Aledár *Orpheus* 1900 Budapest: Nemzeti Múzeum.

KELLER Albert von *In the Moonlight* 1894 private collection. *Love* 1908 lost (survives in photographs).

KHNOPFF Fernand *Caresses* 1896 Brussels: Musées Royaux des Beaux-Arts.

KLIMT Gustav *Judith I* 1901 Vienna: Österreichische Gallerie, Prague: Národní Galerie. *Judith II* (Salome) 1909 Venice: Galleria d'Arte Moderna (Ca' Pesaro).

KOKOSCHKA Oskar *Pietà* 1908 Vienna: Österreichisches Museum Angewandter Künste. *Murderer, Hope of Women* 1909 New York: Museum of Modern Art.

KOVÁCS Margit *Salome* 1943–44, *Kádár Kata* 1962, *Death* 1968 Szentendre: Kovács Múzeum.

LACOMBE Georges *Love* 1894–96 Paris: Musée d'Orsay.

LAGRENÉE Louis *Pygmalion and Galatea* 1781 Detroit: Institute of Arts.

LA LYRE Adolphe *Mary Magdalen* 1892 Blois: Château de Blois.

LANFRANCO Giovanni *The Magdalen Transported to Heaven* c. 1605 Naples: Galleria Nazionale di Capodimonte.

LANTOS Györgyi *Salome* 1985 Budapest: Gulácsy Galerie.

LEFÈBVRE Jules Joseph *Mary Magdalen* 1876 Leningrad: Hermitage.

LEIGHTON Frederic *The Reconciliation of the Montagues and the Capulets* c. 1853–55 Decatur (Georgia): Agnes Scott College. *Paolo and Francesca* c. 1860–61 Hyderabad: Salar Jung Museum. *Orpheus and Eurydice* c. 1864 London: Leighton House Art Gallery and Museum. *Ariadne* 1868 Andhra Pradesh, Hyderabad: Salar Jung Museum. *Summer Moon* 1872 India: private collection. *Summer Slumber* c. 1894 India: private collection. *Flaming June* c. 1895 Puerto Rico: Museo de Arte de Ponce.

LE MOYNE François *Pygmalion* 1729 Tours: Musée des Beaux-Arts.

LÉVY Émile *Zenobia Found by Shepherds* 1850 Paris: École des Beaux-Arts. *The Death of Orpheus* 1866 Paris: Musée d'Orsay.

LÉVY-DHURMER Lucien *Medusa* 1897 Paris: Musée du Louvre.

LEWIS John Frederick *The Siesta* 1876 London: Tate Gallery.

LIEBERMANN Max *Judith* 1917 [Weinmüller, Munich, 1963, Cat. 93, No. 1533].

LINDSAY Norman *Pollice verso* 1904 Melbourne: National Gallery of Victoria. *The Crucified Venus* drawing 1912 Melbourne: National Gallery of Victoria.

LÖFFTZ Ludwig von *Lamentation of Christ by the Magdalen* 1883 Munich: Neue Pinakothek.

MAES-CANINI Jean Baptiste Louis *The Penitent Magdalen* c. 1822 Florence: Galleria d'Arte Moderna.

MAFFEI Francesco *Perseus and Medusa* early 1650s Venice: Accademia.

MAKART Hans *The Death of Cleopatra* 1874–75 Kassel: Staatliche Kunstsammlungen.

MANGUE Jean Marie *Icarus* 1887 Montpellier: Musée Fabre.

MANTEGNA Andrea *Dead Christ* c. 1490 Milan: Brera.

MARTINI Arturo *Ophelia* 1933 Milan: Brera.

MASSYS Jan *Judith* 1543 Rome: Palazzo Barberini.

MASTER OF SAINT BARTHOLOMEW *Descent from the Cross* c. 1500 Paris: Musée du Louvre.

MAX Gabriel von *The Anatomist* 1869 Munich: Neue Pinakothek. *The Resurrection of the Daughter of Jairus* 1878 Montreal: Musée des Beaux-Arts.

MEHUS Lieven *The Three Magdalens* c. 1660 Florence: Depositi delle Gallerie.

MEIT Conrad *Judith* c. 1525–28 Munich: Bayerisches Nationalmuseum.

MICHELANGELO Buonarotti *Pietà* c. 1500 Rome: Saint Peter's, 1555–64 Milan: Castello Sforzesco.

MILLAIS John Everett *Ophelia* 1851–52 London: Tate Gallery.

MINNE George *Pietà* 1929 Brussels: Musées Royaux des Beaux-Arts.

MOORE Albert *Beads* c. 1875 Edinburgh: National Gallery of Scotland. *Apples* 1875 England: Mrs. J. A. Newcomer. *Dreamers* 1882 Birmingham: City Museum and Art Gallery. *Midsummer* 1887 Bournemouth: Russell-Cotes Art Gallery.

MORALES Luis de *Pietà* c. 1553 Badajos: cathedral, c. 1560 Madrid: Prado, mid-1560s Bilbao: Sota, Ducy-Sainte-Marguerite (France): parish church, Barcelona: I. de Balanzó, late 1560s Polán: Alonzo, Badajos: Vizconde del Parque, Malaga: cathedral, Madrid: private collection, Madrid: Academia de San Fernando, Madrid: Palacio Episcopal.

MORAZZONE Pier Francesco *The Magdalen Transported to Heaven* c. 1611 Varese: Basilica di San Vittore.

MOREAU Gustave *The Suitors* 1852–98 Paris: Musée Gustave Moreau. *The Young Man and Death* 1856–65 Cambridge (Massachusetts): Fogg Museum of Art. *A Maenad with the Head of Orpheus* several versions 1865–98 Paris: Louvre, Musée d'Orsay, Musée Gustave Moreau. *The Apparition* 1874–76 Paris: Musée Gustave Moreau. *Salome Dancing* 1876 Paris: Musée Gustave Moreau. *Orpheus on Eurydice's Tomb* 1890 Paris: Musée d'Orsay. *The Bride of the Night* c. 1892 France: Baroness de Goldschmidt.

MUCHA Alphonse *Lying Model* 1904 Prague: City Museum.

MÜLLER Victor *Romeo and Juliet* c. 1870 Augsburg: Staatsgalerie.

MUNCH Edvard *The Scream* pastel 1893 Oslo: Nasjonalgalleriet. *Madonna* 1893–94 Hamburg: Kunsthalle and Oslo: Nasjonalgalleriet. *Vampire* c. 1894 private collection. *The Dead Loving Couple* 1896–97 Oslo: Munch-museet. *The Dance of Life* 1899–1900 Oslo: Nasjonalgalleriet. *Marat* 1905–8 Oslo: Munch-museet.

MUNRO Alexander *Paolo and Francesca* 1851–52 Birmingham: Birmingham Museum and Art Gallery.

OGGIONO Marco d' *The Magdalen Transported to Heaven* 1520s Florence: Galleria degli Uffizi.

PICOT François Édouard *Amor and Psyche* 1817 Paris: Musée du Louvre.

PIGNONI Simone *The Magdalen* c. 1640–60 Florence: Galleria Palatina and Boston: Museum of Fine Arts.

PIRNER Maximilián *Remorse* c. 1885 Prague: Anežský areál. *Nymphs beside a Fountain* 1895 Prague: Anežský areál. *The Stream* 1902 Prague: Anežský areál.

PISANELLO *Study of Hanged Man* early 1430s New York: Frick Collection. *Study of Hanged Man, a Lady, and a Boy* early 1430s London: British Museum. *The Legend of Saint George* 1433–38 Verona: San Giorgietto.

PONTIKER Hans *Salome* 1958 Innsbruck: Ferdinandeum.

PONTORMO Jacopo *Pygmalion* 1529–30 Florence: Palazzo Vecchio.

PRÉAULT Auguste *Ophelia* 1842/70 Paris: Musée d'Orsay.

PRETI Mattia *The Death of Dido* c. 1655 Chambéry: Musée des Beaux-Arts, Braunschweig: Herzog Anton Ulrich Museum.

PREVIATI Gaetano *Paolo and Francesca* 1901 Ferrara: Galleria Civica d'Arte Moderna. *Agony* 1901 Rome: Galleria Nazionale di Arte Moderna.

PRUD'HON Pierre Paul *Phrosine and Mélidore* 1798 Paris: Musée du Louvre. *Justice and Divine Vengeance Pursuing Crime* 1815–18 Paris: Musée du Louvre. *Crucifixion* 1822 Paris: Musée du Louvre.

PUVIS DE CHAVANNE Pierre *Death and the Maidens* 1872 Williamstown: Clark Art Institute.

RAMOS Mel *Señorita Rio—The Queen of Spies* 1963 New York: Louis K. Meisel Gallery.

RAOUX Jean *Pygmalion* 1717 Montpellier: Musée Fabre.

RAVESTEYN Jan Van *Pygmalion and Galatea* c. 1625 New Haven: J. M. Montias.

REDON Odilon *Ophelia with Her Eyes Closed* 1901–2 Almen: Bonger Collection, 1905–6 Paris: Kapferer, New York: Woodner. *Ophelia among the Flowers* 1905 London: National Gallery, Paris: Parent, Mottart, de Hauke, New York: Lasker. *Ophelia the Bride* 1906–8 Domecy: Baroness Domecy, Geneva: Imbert, New York: Slatkin. *Ophelia* 1908–9 Paris: Bacou. *Orpheus* c. 1903 Cleveland: Cleveland Museum of Art.

RENI Guido *The Death of Cleopatra* c. 1626 Potsdam-Sanssouci: Staatliche Schlösser und Gärten, c. 1628–30 Hampton: Hampton Court (Royal Collection), 1639 Florence: Palazzo Pitti, c. 1640–42 Rome: Pinacoteca Capitolana.

RIBOT Théodule *The Martyrdom of Saint Sebastian* 1865 Paris: Musée d'Orsay.

RICCI Sebastiano *Pygmalion* c. 1717 Ruvigliana (Switzerland): Rudolf Heinemann.

RIDEL Louis *Shipwrecked (L'épave)* 1907 lost.

ROBERT-FLEURY Tony *The Last Days of Corinth* 1870 Paris: Musée du Louvre.

ROBINSON Henry Peach *Fading Away* 1858 London: Royal Photographic Society of Great Britain.

ROCHEGROSSE George *The Last Days of Babylon* 1891 lost.

RODIN Auguste *Pygmalion* 1889 Paris: Musée Rodin. *Paolo and Francesca* 1894 Paris: Musée Rodin. *Christ and the Magdalen* c. 1894 San Francisco: Fine Arts Museum.

ROMANINO Girolamo *Pietà* 1535–40 Brescia: Pinacoteca.

ROSSELLI Matteo *The Magdalen and the Redeemer* c. 1650 Colle Val d'Elsa: Museo di Arte Sacra.

ROSSETTI Dante Gabriel *Paolo and Francesca da Rimini* 1855 London: Tate Gallery, 1862 Bedford: Cecil Higgins Art Gallery. *Mary Magdalen at the Door of Simon the Pharisee* 1858 Cambridge: Fitzwilliam Museum. *Beata Beatrix* c. 1863 London: Tate Gallery, 1872 Chicago: Art Institute. *Helen of Troy* 1863 Hamburg: Kunsthalle. *Venus Verticordia* 1864 Bournemouth: Russell-Cotes Art Gallery. *Lady Lilith* 1864 Wilmington (Delaware): Wilmington Society of Fine Arts. *The Bower Meadow* 1872 Manchester: City Art Gallery. *Proserpine* 1872 London: Tate Gallery. *The Blessed Damozel* 1877 Cambridge (Massachusetts): Fogg Museum of Art. *A Sea-Spell* 1877 Cambridge (Massachusetts): Fogg Museum of Art. *Astarte Syriaca* 1877 Manchester: City Art Gallery. *The Daydream* 1880 London: Victoria and Albert Museum.

ROSSO Giovanni Battista [Rosso Fiorentino] *Deposition* 1517 Volterra: Pinacoteca. *Dead Christ with Angels* c. 1526 Boston: Museum of Fine Arts. *The Death of Cleopatra* c. 1528 Braunschweig: Herzog Anton Ulrich Museum. *Pietà* 1530–35 Paris: Musée du Louvre.

ROUAULT Georges *Dead Christ Mourned by Holy Women* 1893 Grenoble: Musée de Grenoble. *Christ on the Cross* 1913 Switzerland: private collection, 1930 private collection, 1935 Hem (France): Philippe Leclercq. *Crucifixion* 1918 Philadelphia: Henry P. McIlhenny, c. 1939 Paris: private collection.

RUBENS Peter Paul *Judith* c. 1606–7 Braunschweig: Herzog Anton Ulrich Museum. *The Death of Adonis in the Arms of Venus* c. 1612 London: British Museum.

SALOMÉ *Judith and Holofernes* 1981 private collection.

SAMMARTINO Giuseppe *Christ under a Shroud* 1753 Naples: Cappella Sansevero.

SARTORIO Giulio Aristide *Diana of Ephesus and the Slaves* c. 1899 Rome: Galleria Nazionale.

SCHEFFER Ary *Paolo and Francesca* c. 1822 Dordrecht: Dordrechts Muzeum, 1854 Paris: Musée du Louvre. *Lenore: The Return from the Army* 1829 Guéret: Musée Municipal. *Lenore: The Dead Ride Fast* 1830 Lille: Musée des Beaux-Arts.

SCHNORR VON CAROLSFELD Ludwig *Leap from the Cliff* 1833 Nuremberg: Germanisches Nationalmuseum.

SCHOENEWERK Alexandre *The Tarantian Maiden* 1871 Paris: Musée d'Orsay.

SELLEMOND Peter *Dance of Death* 1936 Innsbruck: Ferdinandeum.

SERVAES Albert *Pietà* 1920 Brussels: Musées Royaux des Beaux-Arts.

SIRANI Elisabetta *The Magdalen Scourging Herself* 1663 Besançon: Musée des Beaux-Arts.

SLEVOGT Max *Self-Portrait before the Easel with Judith's Picture* 1898/1907 London: K. Steiner. *Sardanapalus* 1907 Hannover: Niedersächsische Landesgalerie. *Golgotha* 1952 Ludwigshafen: Friedenskirche.

SODOMA(?) *Penitent Magdalen* c. 1540s Melbourne (Derbyshire): Lt. Col. Sir Howard and Lady Kerr, the Dower House.

SOLANA José Gutiérrez *The End of the World* c. 1932 Madrid: Conceptión Prieto.

SOLE Gian Gioseffo dal *Mary Magdalen* c. 1700 Verona: Castelvecchio.

STROBL Zsigmond Kisfaludy *David* 1912 Budapest: Nemzeti Múzeum.

STROZZI Bernardo *Salome* early 1630s Berlin-Dahlem: Gemäldegalerie.

STUCK Franz von *Pietà* 1891 Frankfurt: Städelsches Kunstinstitut. *Orpheus* 1891 private collection. *Sin* 1893 Munich: Neue Pinakothek.

TAILLASSON Jean Joseph *Hero and Leander* 1798 Blaye: Musée d'Histoire et d'Art.

TASSAERT Octave *Pygmalion* 1855 Paris: Musée du Louvre.

TERWESTEN Matthäus *Pygmalion* 1700–20 New Haven: J. M. Montias.

TIEPOLO Giambattista *David and the Head of Goliath* c. 1715 Vancouver: Vancouver Art Gallery.

TITIAN *The Magdalen* c. 1531–35 Florence: Galleria Palatina.

TOOROP Jan *Lenore* 1891 Brussels: Musées Royaux des Beaux-Arts.

TROGER Paul *Annointing of Christ's Corpse* c. 1730–38 Innsbruck: Ferdinandeum.

TRÜBNER Wilhelm *The Dead Christ* 1874 Hamburg: Kunsthalle.

TURA Cosmè *The Corpse of Christ Held by Angels* c. 1475 Vienna: Kunsthistorisches Museum. *Pietà* c. 1475 Paris: Musée du Louvre, Venice: Museo Correr.

TURCHI Alessandro *Christ in the Sepulcher* c. 1617–19 Rome: Galleria Borghese. *The Death of Cleopatra* 1635 Paris: Musée du Louvre.

TURNER Joseph Mallord William *The Parting of Hero and Leander* 1837 London: National Gallery.

VASSELON Marius *The Penitent Magdalen* 1887 Tours: Musée des Beaux-Arts.

VASZARY János *Nude Redhead* c. 1910 Budapest: Nemzeti Múzeum.

VERNET Horace *The Ballad of Lenore* 1839 Nantes: Musée des Beaux-Arts.

WALLIS Henry *Chatterton* 1855–56 London: Tate Gallery.

WATSON Homer *The Death of Elaine* 1877 Toronto: Art Gallery of Ontario.

WATTS George Frederick *Found Drowned* 1849–50 Compton (Surrey): Watts Gallery. *Paolo and Francesca* 1872–84 Compton (Surrey): Watts Gallery. *Mammon* 1884–85 London: Tate Gallery. *Love Triumphant* 1899–1900 London: Tate Gallery.

WERFF Adriaen Van der *Mary Magdalen* 1707 Schleißheim: Gemäldegalerie, c. 1710 Dresden: Gemäldegalerie, 1720 Leningrad: Hermitage.

WEST Benjamin *Venus Lamenting the Death of Adonis* c. 1763–67 private collection, 1768/1819 Pittsburgh: Carnegie Institute Museum of Art, 1803 New

Brunswick: Rutgers Art Gallery. *The Death of Hyacinthus* 1771 Swarthmore: Swarthmore College.

WIERTZ Antoine *La belle Rosine* 1847 Brussels: Musée Wiertz. *Buried Alive* 1854 Brussels: Musée Wiertz.

WOESTIJNE Gustaaf Van de *Jesus Christ Offering Us His Blood* 1925 Brussels: Musées Royaux des Beaux-Arts.

WTEWAEL Joachim Antonisz *The Death of Procris* c. 1595 Saint Louis: Art Museum.

Special Credits for Illustrations

Jacket and 41: Friends of Art Museum Fund, Spencer Museum of Art. Frontispiece: on permanent loan to Kassel from the Federal Republic of Germany. 2, 7, and 10: photographs © Art Resource, New York. 3, 11, 42, and 68: photographs © A. C. L., Brussels. 4: Anne-Marie Gillion Crowet, Brussels. 5: gift of Mary King to the Art Gallery of Toronto. 6, 12, 14, 15, and 17: photographs © R. M. N., Paris. 23, 43: bequest, gift of Grenville L. Winthrop to the Fogg Art Museum. 25: photograph by Fabbio Lensini. 30, 32, and 52: photographs © B. P. Keiser. 35: gift of Louis C. Raegner to the Metropolitan Museum of Art. 37: on loan from the Gottfried Keller Foundation to the Kunsthaus, Zurich. 47: photograph by Roland Gretler. 48 and 70: edited by Stephen R. Bissette, SpiderBaby Publications. 51: William Sturgis Bigelow Collection. 56: © 1992 ARS, New York/SPADEM, Paris. 57: gift of Julius S. Morgan. 63: Charles Potter Kling Fund. 65: gift of Alma de Bretteville Spreckels to the Fine Arts Museum of San Francisco. 69 and 71: courtesy of DC Comics, New York. 72: photograph by Steve Lopez. 73 and 77: © Marvel Entertainment Group, New York. 74: © Harris Publications, New York.

Secondary Sources

(Primary sources are identified and dated at the place of citation.)

ARIÈS Philippe *Essais sur l'histoire de la mort en Occident du Moyen Âge à nos jours.* Paris: Seuil, 1975; *L'homme devant la mort.* 2 vols. Paris: Seuil, 1977; *Images de l'homme devant la mort.* 2 vols. Paris: Seuil, 1983.

BENDINER Kenneth *An Introduction to Victorian Painting.* New Haven: Yale University Press, 1985.

BENTLEY Christopher "The Monster in the Bedroom: Sexual Symbolism in Bram Stoker's *Dracula*" in Margaret L. Carter, ed. *Dracula: The Vampire and the Critics.* Ann Arbor: University of Michigan Press, 1988. 25–34.

BINION Rudolph *Frau Lou: Nietzsche's Wayward Disciple.* Princeton, N.J.: Princeton University Press, 1968; *Soundings Psychohistorical and Psycholiterary.* New York: Psychohistory Press, 1981; *After Christianity.* Durango, Colo.: Logbridge-Rhodes, 1986.

BIRKETT Jennifer *The Sins of the Fathers: Decadence in France, 1870–1914.* London: Quartet, 1986.

BLOCH Maurice, and PARRY Jonathan, eds. *Death and the Regeneration of Life.* Cambridge, England: Cambridge University Press, 1982.

BOIS Jules *Le satanisme et la magie.* Paris: Chailley, 1895.

BORZELLI Angelo *Storia della vita e delle opere di Giovan Battista Marino.* Rev. ed. Naples: Artiginelli, 1929.

BOUSQUET Jacques *Les thèmes du rêve dans la littérature romantique (France, Angleterre, Allemagne): Essai sur la naissance et l'évolution des images.* Paris: Didier, 1964.

BUGLIOSI Vincent *Helter Skelter.* New York: Norton, 1974.

BUISINE Alain "Prose tombale" *Revue des sciences humaines* (1975): 539–51. Numéro spécial "Naturalisme."

CALMET Dom Augustin *Dissertation sur les apparitions des anges, des démons, et des esprits et sur les revenans et vampires de Hongrie, de Bohème, de Moravie, et de Silésie.* Paris: De Bure, 1746.

CLARK James M. *The Dance of Death in the Middle Ages and the Renaissance.* Glasgow: Jackson, 1950.

COHEN Kathleen *Metamorphosis of a Death Symbol.* Berkeley: University of California Press, 1973.

COLLIN DE PLANCY Jacques *Dictionnaire infernal.* Paris: Plon, 1818, 1863.

COMINI Alessandra "Vampires, Virgins, and Voyeurs in Imperial Vienna" in Thomas B. Hess and Linda Nochlin, eds. *Woman as Sex Object: Studies in Erotic Art, 1730–1970.* New York: Newsweek, 1972. 207–21.

DAFFNER Hugo *Salome: Ihre Gestalt in Geschichte und Kunst—Dichtung, bildende Kunst, Musik.* Munich: Schmidt, 1912.

DARMENT Richard "The Loved One: Alfred Gilbert's *Mors Janua Vitae*" in Minneapolis Institute of Arts *Victorian High Renaissance.* Minneapolis: Minneapolis Institute of Art, 1978. 42–52.

DELENDA Odile, and MELNOTTE Colette *L'iconographie de Sainte Madeleine après le Concile de Trente: Essai de catalogue des peintures dans les collections publiques françaises.* Ecole du Louvre, Paris, 1984 (exhibition catalogue).

DIJKSTRA Bram *Idols of Perversity: Fantasies of Feminine Evil in Fin-de-Siècle Culture.* New York: Oxford University Press, 1986.

EGGUM Arne "The Theme of Death" in National Gallery of Art *Edvard Munch: Symbols and Images.* Washington, D.C.: National Gallery of Art, 1978. 143–83.

ELLMANN Richard *Oscar Wilde.* New York: Random House, 1988.

ÉPAULARD Alexis *Vampirisme: Nécrophilie, nécrosadisme, nécrophagie.* Lyon: Storck, 1901.

FIEDLER Leslie *Love and Death in the American Novel.* Rev. ed. New York: Stein and Day, 1966.

GAGNIER Regenia "Evolution and Information, or Eroticism and Everyday Life, in *Dracula* and Late Victorian Aestheticism" in Regina Barreca, ed. *Sex and Death in Victorian Literature.* Bloomington: Indiana University Press, 1990. 140–57.

GRIFFIN Gail B. " 'Your Girls That You All Love Are Mine': *Dracula* and the Victorian Male Sexual Imagination" in Margaret L. Carter, ed. *Dracula: The Vampire and the Critics.* Ann Arbor: University of Michigan Press, 1988. 137–48.

HARTMANN Wolfgang "Dante's Paolo and Francesca als Liebespaar" in *Beiträge zur Kunst des 19. und 20. Jahrhunderts* Schweizerisches Institut für Kunstgeschichte: Jahrbuch 1968/69 (1970), 7–24.

HAUSAMANN Torsten *Die tanzende Salome in der Kunst von der christlichen Frühzeit bis um 1500*: Ikonographische Studien. Zurich: Juris, 1980.

HENTIG Hans von *Der nekrotrope Mensch: Vom Totenglauben zur morbiden Totennähe.* Stuttgart: Enke, 1964.

HERTZ Robert "La représentation collective de la mort" (1907) *Mélanges de sociologie religieuse et folklore.* Paris: Alcan, 1928.

HESSISCHES LANDESMUSEUM DARMSTADT *Memento mori: Der Tod als Thema der Kunst vom Mittelalter bis zur Gegenwart.* Darmstadt: Hessisches Landesmuseum, 1984 (exhibition catalogue).

HIRSCHFELD Magnus *Geschlechtsanomalien und Perversionen.* Paris: Chapireau [1953].

HOCK Stefan *Die Vampyrsagen und ihre Verwertung in der deutschen Literatur.* Berlin: Duncker, 1900.

HOFMANN Werner, ed. *Zauber der Medusa: Europäische Manierismen.* Vienna: Löcker, 1987.

HONOUR Hugh *Romanticism.* New York: Harper and Row, 1979.

HUIZINGA Johan *The Waning of the Middle Ages.* London: Arnold, 1924.

HUNTINGTON Richard, and METCALF Peter *Celebrations of Death.* Cambridge, England: Cambridge University Press, 1979.

INGENHOFF-DANHÄUSER Monika *Maria Magdalena: Heilige und Sünderin der italienischen Renaissance.* Tübingen: Wasmuth, 1984.

JONES Ernest *On the Nightmare.* London: Hogarth/Institute of Psycho-analysis, 1931.

JULLIAN Philippe *Esthètes et magiciens: L'art fin de siècle.* Paris: Perrin, 1969.

KEULS Eva C. *The Reign of the Phallus: Sexual Politics in Ancient Athens.* New York: Harper and Row, 1985.

KINGSBURY Martha "The Femme Fatale and Her Sisters" in Thomas B. Hess and Linda Nochlin, eds. *Woman as Sex Object: Studies in Erotic Art, 1730–1970.* New York: Newsweek, 1972. 183–205.

LEGMAN Gershon *Love and Death.* New York: Hacker, 1949, 1963.

LEVIN William R. *Images of Love and Death in Late Medieval and Renaissance Art* catalogue University of Michigan Museum of Art exhibition 21 November 1975–4 January 1976.

LINSE Ulrich "Über den Prozeß der Syphilisation: Körper und Sexualität um 1900 in ärztlicher Sicht" in A. Schiller and N. Heim, eds. *Vermessene Sexualität.* Berlin: Springer, 1987.

McCLELLAND David C. *The Roots of Consciousness*. Princeton, N.J.: Van Nostrand, 1964.

McDANNELL Colleen, and LENZ Bernhard *Heaven: A History*. New Haven: Yale University Press, 1988.

MacKAY Carol Hanbery "Controlling Death and Sex: Magnification v. the Rhetoric of Rules in Dickens and Thackeray" in Regina Barreca, ed. *Sex and Death in Victorian Literature*. Bloomington: Indiana University Press, 1990. 120–39.

MAIGRON Louis *Le romantisme et les moeurs*. Paris: Champion, 1910.

MÂLE Émile *L'art religieux de la fin du XVIe siècle, du XVIIe siècle et du XVIIIe siècle: Étude sur l'iconographie après le Concile de Trente*. Paris: Colin, 1932, 1951.

MINNEAPOLIS INSTITUTE OF ARTS *Victorian High Renaissance*. 1986 (exhibition catalogue).

MITCHELL Allan "Philippe Ariès and the French Way of Death" in *French Historical Studies* X (Fall 1978): 684–95.

MITTERAND Henri "Étude" in Émile Zola *Les Rougon–Macquart IV*. Paris: Gallimard, 1966. 1710–58.

MOSCO Marilena, ed. *La Maddalena tra sacro e profano*. Florence: Usher, 1986 (exhibition catalogue).

PEUCHET Jacques *Mémoires tirés des archives de la police de Paris pour servir à l'histoire de la morale et de la police*. 6 vols. Paris: Levavasseur, 1838.

PFISTER Oskar *Die Frömmigkeit des Grafen Ludwig von Zinzendorf*. Leipzig: Deuticke, 1925.

PICHON Yann le *L'érotisme des chers maîtres*. Paris: Denoël, 1986.

PRAZ Mario *La carne, la morte e il diavolo nella letteratura romantica*. Florence: Sansoni, 1930, 1942, 1976. *The Romantic Agony*. London: Oxford University Press, 1933, 1951, 1970.

PROELSS Robert *Heinrich Heine*. Stuttgart: Rieger, 1886.

REIMARUS SECUNDUS (pseud.) *Geschichte der Salome von Cato bis Oscar Wilde*. 3 vols. Leipzig: Wigand, 1913.

RIPA Cesare *Iconologia*. Rome: Giliotti, 1595.

SILVERMAN Debora L. *Art Nouveau in Fin-de-Siècle France: Politics, Psychology, and Style*. Berkeley: University of California Press, 1989.

STEINBERG Leo *Other Criteria*. New York: Oxford University Press, 1972.

STUMP Jeanne "The Sculpture of Émile Hébert: Themes and Variations" in *The Register of the Spencer Museum of Art* V, no. 10 (Spring 1982): 25–61.

SUMMERS Montague *The Vampire: His Kith and Kin*. London: Paul, Trench, and Trubner, 1928.

TAXIL Léo *La prostitution contemporaine: Étude d'une question sociale*. Paris: Librairie populaire [1884]; *La corruption fin de siècle*. Paris: Noirot, 1894.

TENENTI Alberto *La vie et la mort à travers l'art du XVe siècle.* Paris: Colin, 1952; *Il senso della morte e l'amore della vita nel Rinascimento (Francia e Italia).* Turin: Einaudi, 1957; *Credenze, ideologie, libertinismi tra Medioevo ed Età moderna.* Bologna: Il Mulino, 1978.

TERRY Maury *The Ultimate Evil.* Garden City, N.Y.: Doubleday, 1987.

THIER Ludger, and CALUFETTI Abele, eds. *Il libro della beata Angela da Foligno.* Grottoferrata (Rome): Editiones Collegii S. Bonaventurae ad Claras Aquas, 1985.

THOMAS Louis Vincent *Le cadavre.* Brussels: Complexe, 1980.

TINTNER Adeline R. *The Museum World of Henry James.* Ann Arbor: University of Michigan Press, 1986.

TRACY Robert "Loving You All Ways: Vamps, Vampires, Necrofiles, and Necrofilles in Nineteenth-Century Fiction" in Regina Barreca, ed. *Sex and Death in Victorian Literature.* Bloomington: Indiana University Press, 1990. 32–59.

TWITCHELL James B. *The Living Dead: A Study of the Vampire in Romantic Literature.* Durham, N.C.: Duke University Press, 1981; "The Vampire Myth" in Margaret L. Carter, ed. *Dracula: The Vampire and the Critics.* Ann Arbor: University of Michigan Press, 1988. 109–16.

VERMEULE Emily *Aspects of Death in Early Greek Art and Poetry.* Berkeley: University of California Press, 1979.

VETTER Ingeborg *Das Erbe der 'Schwarzen Romantik' in der deutschen Décadence: Studien zur 'Horrorgeschichte' um 1900.* Inaugural-Dissertation (Graz) 1976.

VILLENEUVE Roland, and DEGAUDENZI Jean Louis *Le musée des vampires.* Paris: Veyrier, 1976.

VOVELLE Michel *La mort et l'Occident de 1300 à nos jours.* Paris: Gallimard, 1983.

WIRTH Jean *La jeune fille et la mort: Recherches sur les thèmes macabres dans l'art germanique de la Renaissance.* Geneva: Droz, 1979.

ZENTRALINSTITUT FÜR SEPULKRALKULTUR DER ARBEITSGEMEINSCHAFT FRIEDHOF UND DENKMAL e.V. *Freund Hein und der Bücherfreund: Ex libris des 20. Jahrhunderts aus der Sammlung des Zentralinstituts für Sepulkralkultur.* Kassel [1986] (exhibition catalogue).

Index

(Italicized page numbers refer to illustrations or quotations. For individual works, see their authors' names.)